Raising a Child Who Has a Physical Disability

Donna G. Albrecht

Foreword by Robert Miller, M.D.,
Chair, Department of Neurology,
California Pacific Medical Center

John Wiley & Sons, Inc.
New York · Chichester · Brisbane · Toronto · Singapore

For Abby, Katie, and especially Mike, without whom this book could not have been written.

■ ■ ■

This text is printed on acid-free paper.

Copyright © 1995 by Donna G. Albrecht.

Published by John Wiley & Sons, Inc.

All rights reserved. Published simultaneously in Cananda.

Library of Congress Cataloging-in-Publication Data

Albrecht, Donna G.
    Raising a child who has a physical disability / Donna G. Albrecht.
      p. cm.
    Includes bibliographical references and index.
    ISBN 0-471-04240-4
    1. Physically handicapped children—United States. 2. Physically
handicapped children—United States—Family relationships.
3. Parents of handicapped children—United States. I. Title.
HV904.A5   1995
649'.151—dc20   94-41908

Printed in the United States of America.

10 9 8 7 6 5 4 3 2 1

Contents

Acknowledgments

My two decades of parenting have given me a deep respect for the generosity of parents whose children have physical disabilities and the professionals who work with us. I say "us" because my husband and I were blessed with two extraordinary daughters, Katie and Abby, who both were born with a neuromuscular condition.

Many families have shared their experiences and expertise during interviews for this book and they have my deepest thanks. Some identifying details of their stories have been changed to protect their privacy and I will not be naming them here for the same reason. I believe their experiences will be helpful to others, but I have very strong personal reservations about writing anything that could ever make these generous families, and especially their children, uncomfortable if they were identified.

Many fine associations and government offices were also instrumental in helping me get the most up-to-date information to include in this book. You will find most of those organizations listed in the appendixes. In addition, I would like to thank: The National Association of Private Schools for Exceptional Children, the Association for the Care of Children's Health, Designs for Change, and *Exceptional Parent* magazine.

I owe a debt of gratitude to some skilled professionals who shared their expertise with me, and through this book, with you. They include Lawrence Frolik, Jack Davies, Ann Marie Robinson, Dr. Birt Harvey, Debra Flanders, and Bonnie Holaday.

My thanks to my editor PJ Dempsey at John Wiley & Sons, Inc., who recognized the need for this book and helped make it a reality. Thanks, too, to Nana Prior whose editorial expertise has been invaluable.

Finally, special thanks to Dr. Robert Miller for writing the Foreword to this book. He is an extraordinarily skilled physician and medical researcher who is also a warm, kind, and generous human being. My family has had the pleasure of knowing him and the great benefit of his medical expertise for many years and we are grateful.

Foreword

In 20 years of caring for children with neuromuscular diseases, I have never encountered a more effective parent than Donna Albrecht. She quickly developed a wisdom and expertise balanced with humor and love that has set an example for many other parents and families. Over the years, she has been a help to many parents who were just beginning to adjust to life with a child who is physically disabled. What comes through loud and clear in *Raising a Child Who Has a Physical Disability* is the tremendous experience and wisdom gleaned both from her own personal experience and from the close sharing with numerous other parents and families.

After over two decades of personal experience with two children who were born with substantial physical limitations, Donna has impressive credentials to produce this volume. She speaks with the voice of a real expert.

Many areas she covers in this book deserve special attention from the reader. The section on seeking diagnostic help and obtaining additional medical opinions is especially useful to the families who are only just beginning to discover the medical ramifications of their child's disability. Even more important is the subsequent section on coming to grips with the medical diagnosis and the emotional up-heaval that is generated in that difficult time.

It is a fact of life that families frequently find that coping with the special needs of a disabled child can be emotionally traumatic and even lead to the break up of the family. *Raising a Child Who Has a Physical Disability* gives special emphasis to the preservation of a healthy relationship between the parents and also the specific needs of communicating with other friends and family members about the nature of the disability.

Brothers and sisters of disabled children bear a special burden and have very special needs—particularly for effective communication and support. Donna deals clearly and fairly with those needs and gives specific steps that will strengthen the family unit while acknowledging and dealing with the concerns and problems siblings face.

The practical details of choosing the various health care providers that are needed and developing successful, ongoing relationships for a child with a physical disability are very effectively detailed. Health care providers will find this an especially enlightening section as they work to understand and assist with the special needs these families experience.

Developing good self-esteem is a critical developmental step for any child. When a child's life is complicated by a physical disability, social and emotional factors make it much more difficult to develop a healthy self-image. This book gives parents, professionals, and others the tools they need to enable children to develop that positive self-esteem that will carry them through difficult times.

Donna also goes into considerable detail in explaining the problem of getting the best possible education for a child, particularly as it relates to the legal rights provided by the Individuals with Disability Educational Act. Clear, practical advice is given on all the aspects involved in creating and structuring an Individualized Educational Program to meet the unique and individual needs of children who have disabling conditions. Helping professionals who work with these families will find that this section helps them understand the parents' perspective in the process as well as clarify questions they may have about the process itself.

Part of the struggle many families face is identifying and acquiring the specialized equipment their child needs to be able to participate in life to his or her fullest potential. Along with that comes the need to manage the countless details of daily living that become more complicated when the disability and equipment are added to the family. While no one can magically make those complications disappear, *Raising a Child Who Has a Physical Disability* does give valuable pointers on management techniques taken from experiences of families who have lived with the problems, and the stories those families tell often show how humor can help take the sting from the tough times.

Finally, while we live in today, we must all plan for the future. Solid information is given that will assist families, professionals, and caregivers in their long-term planning and goal setting. In addition, there is exploration of some of the choices families face as their children grow and ways to evaluate those choices effectively.

In summary, this book contains a wealth of information for parents, teachers, family members, and health care providers of children who have physical disabilities. I especially recommend it to those providers involved with physical medicine and rehabilitation; general pediatrics; any of the pediatric specialities, including pulmonary medicine, neurology, rheumatology and gastroenterology; as well as orthopedic surgery and neurosurgery, social work, psychology, and psychiatry. Students, residents, and interns with an interest in this field will all benefit immensely from reading this book. It not only offers much on the first reading, but serves as a sourcebook for frequent reference.

I would like to offer my congratulations to Donna Albrecht for *Raising a Child Who Has a Physical Disability*. She can be proud of this tremendous contribution that will help ease the burden of physical disability for many patients and families for years to come.

Robert Miller, M.D.
Chair, Department of Neurology, California Pacific Medical Center,
Clinical Professor of Neurology at the University of California San Francisco,
Muscular Dystrophy Clinic Director and Director of Neuromuscular Research

Introduction

If you are reading this, you probably love a child who has a physical disability. Maybe you are a parent. Perhaps you are another relative, a friend, caregiver, teacher, or therapist, or have some other connection to the child. Welcome.

For the past 20 years, my husband and I have been parents who dealt daily with the issues surrounding disability in childhood. Both of our daughters were born with a neuromuscular disease that is apparent in infancy. Like many of you, we found the early years extremely difficult while we tried to learn everything we could and to do everything possible to take care of our children's physical and emotional needs.

There were times when I felt like I was inventing the wheel as I tried to find the best way to handle different situations. Over time, I discovered that others who had gone before me had already invented a lot of wheels, and they were eager to help make my journey smoother by sharing what they had learned.

Since those early years, I have found myself wearing some rather surprising hats. I have designed and supervised construction of special playgrounds at a school for children with physical disabilities, spent years as a Scout leader, sat on uncounted committees for school activities, helped my city increase handicapped access, and become a professional writer.

Most important to me is that I have had a chance to pass on the instructions for inventing the wheel. Over 10 years ago, my husband and I founded a parent support group under the auspices of the local Muscular Dystrophy Association office. This book was inspired by the parents I have gotten to know through this group, and by the many families throughout North America who have been referred to me by their physicians as a parent to talk with.

This book is full of real-life, nuts-and-bolts information. Some of it is from my personal experience, but much of it is from the experiences of other parents and caregivers. Many of the same concerns and questions come up in conversations with parents who are handling a wide range of physical disabilities in their children. Your situation is unique, but you may be surprised at how much you have in common with other families.

The technical information has been reported as carefully as possible. However, please remember that this book is not intended to substitute for professional advice in any area. For the most up-to-date and personally relevant advice, please consult competent professionals. Throughout the book, I will give you tips for finding professionals whose expertise can help you and your child.

What this book *is* intended to do is help you get a step up when inventing the wheel you need to help the child you love. Use the information in this book. Learn from the medical and other professionals you come in contact with because of your child's disability. Observe your child carefully so you understand her talents, strengths, and needs. When you have done all that, trust your gut. No one knows your child better than you do and no one loves him more than you.

While some writiers use "he" as a generic person and others strive to differentiate by carefully noting gender or saying "he or she," I tend to find these devices somewhat artificial. So, when the gender is not important, I have taken the liberty of plugging in either "he" or "she." When the situation being described sounds similar to something you are dealing with, please feel free to plug in the appropriate pronoun to make the example more relevant to you.

I do confess that I have tended to assume that the primary caregiver for your child is a woman since mothers traditionally fill that role. However, if you are a male who is the primary caregiver, please feel free to change the gender in my examples in your copy of this book wherever you choose.

I want you to know that you are not alone. There are more parents out there who share some parts of your experience than you can possibly imagine. Learn from them now. Then, later, teach the next generation of parents what you have learned and discovered. Your child and all children who have disabilities will be the better for it.

PART I

"Your Child Has a Problem"

1

The Diagnostic Process

Getting Started

While not everyone will have the same tests and evaluations that lead to a diagnosis for their child's disability, there are many stages in the diagnostic process that nearly all parents share. Those stages can include suspecting a problem, preliminary evaluation, specific diagnosis, and development of a medical treatment plan.

Some disabilities, such as spina bifida or cleft palate, are immediately recognizable. When these disabilities are identified, you will probably start the evaluations for treatment before your newborn first goes home from the hospital.

However, the first hints that everything is not perfect often start out as a vague suspicion. There may be unusual delays for a very young baby to reach developmental steps, and it makes you wonder if there could be a problem. Maybe an older child is beginning to have difficulty with motor skills he had mastered long ago, or another child's growth has been so slow that you haven't had to buy new sneakers in nearly two years. Or something else is bothering you.

As a parent, you will often be the first to see signs of a medical condition that must be dealt with. You should always talk with your child's physician about any concerns that you have and expect to receive answers that you understand. If you do not completely understand what the doctor is telling you, you have every right (and actually a responsibility to your child) to keep asking questions until you *do* understand what is going on.

In some cases, your child's physician may be the first to notice that there is a problem that could be a disability. During your child's regular appointments, she will examine your child and compare those results to previous examinations and data about what children his age are normally doing. When your son is not progressing as he should, your child's doctor may want to perform some other tests and evaluations to determine the cause of the abnormal results.

One mother on the East Coast was concerned about her four-year-old daughter's cough, suspecting bronchitis. Not being at home, she took her child to a pediatrician who came highly recommended by a friend. Along with treating the bronchitis, the doctor noted that the girl was off the bottom of the growth chart and had a low hairline on the back of her head. He asked the mother's permission to do some tests.

A few weeks later, the tests came back. Her daughter had Turner's Syndrome, a genetic condition that results in short stature and incomplete sexual maturation. While the condition is not curable, the early diagnosis has given the family time to seek out treatment options and the daughter is currently taking medication to enhance her growth.

What's Next?

When the doctor feels that your child's growth and development are not what they should be, he will tell you what steps he recommends for getting more information. The steps could include watching your child for a period of time to see if he catches up in his development, having tests done to determine the cause of the problem, or referral to a specialist who works with children who have needs similar to those of your child.

In the past, many parents (especially mothers) found that their child's primary care physician would discount their concerns in the early stages. Some were told they were just "too hyper" and their baby would be better if they relaxed more. Others were told that their baby was lazy and would outgrow it.

Fortunately, you are much less likely to be faced with this patronizing attitude today. More and more professionals are realizing that parents are an important part of the medical team—and are in the best position to observe their child over long periods of time and in different settings.

If you find yourself in a situation where you feel you are being patronized and your legitimate concerns about your child's health are not being given the consideration they deserve, you have three choices:

1. Try to talk with the medical professional about how you perceive the relationship working and how you would like to see it changed.

2. If that doesn't work, try for a second opinion (see below).

3. If all else fails, change medical professionals. More on that in chapter 4.

Getting a Specific Diagnosis

In nearly all cases, the doctors will be able to give you a diagnosis once they have run their tests and done their evaluations. However, for a few children, the symptoms and test results may not point to a specific diagnosis right away.

It is incredibly difficult to go for long periods of time knowing that something is wrong with your child but not having a name for it and not knowing the effect the problem will have on your child's health and development. Your doctor may be able to give you some idea of the specific diagnoses he suspects and how those disabilities normally progress or get better.

If your child's doctor is stumped, do not hesitate to ask for a referral to a specialist or a medical clinic that focuses on diagnosing and treating children with similar problems. Local medical schools are often a good place to start looking for expert diagnosticians. The educational component at these facilities tends to challenge all their medical professionals to stay on top of new developments.

Be a Partner in the Diagnostic Process

You can help you child's doctor in the search for a diagnosis. You can:

Keep a notebook of the symptoms and situations that concern you. Note the time of day, the place, the relationship to other activities such as nap or play time, the relationship to meals or snacks, or other details that may provide a clue to doctors.

Read everything you can get your hands on about children and families dealing with similar problems. These books or articles may give you insight into a diagnosis or ways to handle symptoms.

Share your concerns with professionals you come into contact with. They may have information from their experience that will point you in the right direction or put you in contact with other professionals or organizations that will be helpful.

Share your concerns with other parents—especially other parents whose children have physical disabilities. They may be able to refer you to physicians, clinics, or other medical resources that can help you achieve a diagnosis and treatment plan for your child.

Once you have the diagnosis, you may want to continue using the same primary care physician who referred you to the specialists. Good doctors often work in partnership with each other. Your primary physician may consult regularly with the diagnosing specialist, thereby allowing your child to receive state-of-the-art treatment at his (probably) less expensive office.

Again, you have the right and responsibility to understand your child's diagnosis and its ramifications. You also have the right to understand and accept or decline (as permitted by law) treatments the doctors recommend.

I will say this more than once in this book, but only because it is so important: Take a small notebook and write down what the doctor says about your child's diagnosis, the effects the condition will have on your child's future, and the treatment options (including the pros and cons for each).

Even if you normally have a very good memory, you are going through an incredibly stressful time. It is simply not reasonable to expect to remember everything the doctor says, all the new terms, and all the new concepts the first time you hear them. Writing them down gives you the opportunity to go back over them later. In addition, it allows you to share information accurately with your spouse or other family members who were not at the medical appointment, and you can be sure you have all the right terms if you decide to do some library research on the diagnosis.

The Treatment Plan

Once your doctor determines what your child's physical problems are, your first question will probably be, "What can we do to cure her?"

Not every medical problem can be cured. Not all medical problems can even be stabilized. Your doctor can tell you if there is any cure or treatment for your child's condition or if the best that can be done right now is to treat symptoms or peripheral problems (like respiratory infections) as they occur.

You might also want to ask your doctor if any research is being done on this diagnosis, where it is being done, and who is funding it. Some parents decide to work with their doctor to seek out any new research data or to search for experimental programs they may want to consider having their child participate in. Both are especially true in situations where there is no commonly used treatment that has a high success rate.

If your doctor recommends a treatment, take time to ask questions so you are sure you understand it thoroughly. Know (and write down) anything your doctor expects you to help with, such as:

- Timing of meals or medications.
- Restrictions on foods or activities.

- Timing and techniques for therapies.
- What to do if a medication is missed.

Ask about what improvements you can expect to see and what the time frame will be. Ask about any side effects and what to do if they occur.

Your child's doctor may discuss different ways to handle your child's medical needs. Unless you are in an emergency situation, be sure to take as much time as you need to completely understand all the ramifications of each option. In an emergency, you may have to trust your doctor and your gut to tell you what to do. Within legal limits (that your doctor or the social worker at your hospital can explain), you have the right to choose between the treatment options that your doctors suggest.

There is another factor you need to consider. If you know there is some reason why it will be difficult or impossible for you to handle the treatment at home, be honest about it with your child's medical professionals. The doctors may not be aware of the conflicts that occur with your other commitments or financial limitations that may make their plans impossible for you to comply with. No treatment plan will work if you are not able to implement it. When you are open with the doctors, they may help you find other ways to accomplish the same results or there may be other resources that they can help you access to achieve the same result.

Be sure you get training for any techniques you will be expected to perform, such as giving shots, doing physical therapy, or doing tracheal suctioning. Practice those activities on your child, right there in the room with the medical professional who is teaching you, until you are comfortable with your skills.

2

When to Get a Second Opinion

Any time you learn about a potential disability or the possibility of surgical procedures, it is very normal to want a second (or even third) medical opinion.

If you have any uncomfortable feelings that you are not satisfied with the diagnosis or how the doctor arrived at it, consider looking for a second opinion. Also, if the implications of the diagnosis are negative or the treatment entails some risk, you may want another independent opinion to verify the diagnosis. For example, if a child is diagnosed with bone cancer in her arm and the doctor advises that amputation is the best course of treatment, many parents would insist on a second opinion before allowing the surgery to take place.

If you worry that asking for a second opinion might offend your child's physician, don't. Good doctors want you to be completely comfortable with the diagnosis so that you will be able to commit completely to the treatment plan and have confidence in the therapies they recommend. In fact, many doctors will suggest that if you have any questions, you should get another medical opinion. As one doctor said, "It can only help."

When you would like a second opinion, you might start the conversation with something like, "I trust you, but since this is such a major diagnosis/decision, with major implications, I would feel best if I had a second opinion." If you ask, the doctor may also be able to refer you to colleagues who are recognized experts on the kinds of problems your child is facing.

One caution here. There is a world of difference between seeking second or third opinions and "doctor shopping." It's only human to want to keep looking until you find the answer you want to hear. Unfortunately, in that circumstance, you may end up with bad information that could even be dangerous for your child. Whenever you look for another opinion, be sure you look for people who are well-recognized experts at medical schools, teaching hospitals, or service organizations.

When Surgery Is Contemplated

When you have been advised to have nonemergency surgical procedures done on your child, be aware that many insurance plans have provisions for obtaining a second opinion on the surgery, as well as related lab tests, X rays, and other expenses, before permitting coverage. Depending on your policy and the procedures contemplated, getting a second (or third) opinion may be voluntary or mandatory.

The insurance company may pay full expenses, be limited to usual and customary charges for surgical consultations (with no deductible or coinsurance requirement), be limited to usual and customary charges but be subject to deductible or coinsurance provisions, or be subject to a fixed fee if the doctor agrees to accept the fee as payment in full. (In that case, lab fees and related expenses may be paid up to a fixed limit.)

According to the Health Insurance Association of America, even health insurance plans that do not specifically pay for a second surgical opinion may cover expenses for presurgical consultations. Major medical plans often consider second surgical opinions as covered medical expenses and, if so, will cover these expenses as they would any usual and customary expenses, subject to the deductible or coinsurance provisions of the policy.

Under some insurance plans, you may be required to seek a second opinion before elective surgery. If your policy has this mandatory approach, you may find that unless you seek out a second opinion, your policy may not pay the surgical benefit or may reimburse the surgical benefit at a lower level than if you had obtained a second opinion. When the requirement is in force, you, the policyholder, are not obligated to act on the second opinion, just to get it.

Whenever you consider obtaining a second opinion, check with your insurance carrier to determine exactly what expenses will be covered. If you find that you do not have adequate insurance coverage, consider working with your state's programs that assist children who have disabilities or with charities or social service agencies that focus on disabilities similar to your child's [like Shriner's Hospitals (see chapter 5) or the Muscular Dystrophy Association]. Sometimes they have low- or no-cost clinics available to give you an expert second opinion.

3

Learning to Live with It

Accepting and Managing Your Feelings

There is no pain quite like the pain you feel when you discover that your child has a disability. Whether it is evident at birth, a genetic problem that becomes apparent later, or a sudden accident that causes the disability, the emotional burden can overwhelm you, especially in the beginning.

As a parent, the emotions you experience are likely to be the strongest you have ever had—and in some cases the most confusing. You may find yourself managing feelings of grief, anger, and protectiveness all jumbled together with the love. That's normal.

Grieving

Think for a moment of the grieving. You may discover that you are grieving several losses. From your standpoint, you are grieving the loss of the child you thought you had, or dreamed she would become. Perhaps there go the ballet lessons and cheerleader costumes, or maybe the evenings shooting hoops or building soapbox racers together.

While at some level you may feel grief for the rest of your life, it is important to realize that regardless of how long your child lives, today is the only day you can be sure you have. You can choose how to live it.

One of the saddest situations in life is when people spend so much time focusing on the problems brought on by the disability or the eventual death that they miss the joy along the way.

Certainly there can be times when you are overwhelmed with grief and sadness, and you should take time to deal with those feelings. However, if you focus on the here and now most of the time, you and your child will have a better today. Find something you enjoy together whether it is as simple as sharing an ice cream cone and laughing at silly cartoons or something more challenging.

One California family had often played board games. But once the kids got past the preschool level, the parents stopped cheating to make it easier for them. Everyone knew that when they won a game it was because they deserved to win and that made the victory very sweet.

However, the one game their teenage daughter never won was her favorite, Chinese Checkers. Homebound during the last three months before she died of neuromuscular disease, she and her mom must have played hundreds of games, with the daughter telling mom where to move the marbles. Finally, a week before she died, the daughter won two games in a row. It was hard to tell who was more proud, the daughter for finally reaching this goal or the mom for seeing her child live every moment to the fullest—even in the face of death.

Anger

Anger is another very normal reaction to your child's disability. It can come from a variety of sources. Sometimes the anger is directed at yourself or others who you feel may have contributed to your child's problems. Sometimes it is focused on your inability to control the situation and cure your child. Other times it can be focused on God or fate.

When you feel anger, it is very tempting to vent it. While you obviously need to have a way to express these strong feelings, you need to find a safe way to do it. Hopefully, you can talk with your partner and family members or friends. Many parents find it especially helpful to talk with parents facing the same situation, but who have been dealing with it longer. (Tips for finding those parents are in chapter 5.)

When you talk with other parents, you are likely to find that your feelings are not unique. Even the strongest feelings that you may be afraid to admit initially (because you fear they are too unacceptable to think, much less put into words) are frequently shared by others.

It is very common to feel angry with yourself at times. Mothers, especially, can find themselves feeling angry and betrayed by their own bodies if the problem is genetic or a birth defect. There can also be the "what if's," such as what if I hadn't breathed those paint fumes, what if I hadn't had that drink or taken that medication?

Your doctor can help you separate the old myths from the real problems. Then she can refer you to help for any problems you can work on now, such as finding a program to help you stop smoking. Smoking during pregnancy can lead to low-birth-weight babies who may have other problems. If you continue to smoke after the birth, the second-hand smoke your child inhales can contribute to respiratory problems. Your doctor or your child's doctor will be able to help you find programs to give you information and support as you quit your smoking habit.

If you have a continuing problem of anger and blame directed at yourself or your partner, consider asking a physician or the social worker at your medical facility for a referral to a professional therapist or peer counselor who can help you deal with your feelings.

Parents sometimes focus their anger on a third party. Perhaps it is the medical professional who delivered the baby, or an employer who may have maintained an unsafe workplace, or even a pest-control or lawn-maintenance company that the parents feel may have caused toxic exposures. If you experience this type of anger, you should consult medical and legal authorities to decide how, or if, you want to proceed. This can help you cope with your anger and possibly protect others from similar problems.

Protectiveness

It is a very human instinct to try to protect your children from hurt and harm. When your child has a disability, that instinct can be multiplied a hundredfold.

You need to know that your feelings are very normal. But you also need to know that you cannot change reality and there is only so much you can do to keep your child from being hurt and still allow him to have a life of his own.

You will have to strike a balance (that will have to be constantly adjusted over the years). On the one hand, you will want to protect your child; on the other hand, you will want to encourage your child's personal growth and independence.

You may find that in addition to your personal urge to protect your child, people in your family and social network also may tend to reinforce activities that protect your child, even when those activities are in direct contradiction to your child's need to develop independence.

There is no way that you, as a parent, can measure whether your efforts have become overbearing. It will be a judgment call you will have to make day by day. Here are some factors to consider:

- Can my child physically keep up with his goals?
- Can my child handle his goals emotionally?
- Does he ask to attempt independence activities that his peers experience and can he physically and emotionally perform those activites (that is, playing with peers, crossing the street, walking home from school, staying alone at home for a short while, or making phone calls independently)?
- Am I basing my decision on his needs or my fears?

In all likelihood, your urge to give special protection to your child who is disabled will never completely go away. But, if you remember to balance it with your child's need to achieve independence, protectiveness will be a positive feeling, working for your childs' best interests.

One Day at a Time

At times, many parents feel almost paralyzed by fears of the future. The whole situation feels so overwhelming that even simple, every-day activities seem impossibly demanding. It can help to remember that you do not have to do everything today.

You do not have to learn all the medical terms and techniques today.

You do not have to learn how to deal with all the new pro-fessionals your child needs today.

You do not have to find ways to pay for all the equipment your child will need for a lifetime today.

If your child weighs 40 pounds right now, you don't need to worry how you will handle him when he weighs 100—at least not today.

Not spending today worrying about every problem you will ever face is nothing like Scarlett O'Hara saying she'll worry about things tomorrow. You still must cope with *many* things today. You just keep your load of worries at a manageable level by focusing on your problems as they need to be handled.

Caring for your child who is disabled can be compared to learn-ing math in school. No one expected you to do algebra in first grade. You started learning the basics and worked your way up. Start by learning the basics about your child's disability and over time (and as needed) you will learn the other skills you need to know. When you look back in a few months or years, you will be amazed at how far you have come.

One more thought. Part of managing your feelings is taking care of yourself. Give yourself permission to have bad days. You probably thought you cried yourself out when you first learned about your child's disability. But there can be times that creep up on you when those feelings resurface. You have to expect that.

When you give yourself permission to take care of your physical and emotional needs, you will be better able to handle the tough times. In the long run, making yourself a martyr to your child's needs will not benefit either of you. So be sure to get enough rest, eat good food every day, and build a strong support network you can depend on when you need help.

Pulling the Family Together

It is common wisdom that tough times either bring people together or pull them apart. Which do you see for your family?

The ability to stay together as a family depends on many different variables. Some include how committed each of you are to the marriage and family, your spiritual values and how committed you are to them, and the other resources you are able to access.

Before going to extremes to hold your family together, a caveat. Not all families can or should stay together. There are times when one partner's abusiveness or immaturity create an insurmountable obstacle to maintaining the family. There are times when no matter how hard the partners work at it, they are not able to build a mutually supportive relationship. If it becomes necessary to separate or divorce, please make an effort to have both partners keep a good relationship with your child(ren). Every child deserves to be loved and your child with a disability will always have special need of all the care and love he can get from both parents.

Keys to Coping as a Couple

Share Your Feelings. One of the most important things you can do as a couple is share your feelings. It is not easy to give up the dream of the child you thought you had while trying to adjust to the reality of the situation you find yourself living with.

Sometimes one person will try to hold in everything in the hopes of protecting the partner. Unfortunately, it is more likely to make both people feel isolated at a time when they already hurt.

You should also share information. If one parent normally deals with the doctors, schools, and other organizations, it helps to take notes or tape record meetings the other cannot get to. Then spend time after those meetings going over everything together. This can help keep both of you realistic about what is going on.

For example, if you simply say that a therapy evaluation went fine, your partner might think that meant your child was getting much better. In reality, fine to you might mean that your child did not lose as much ground as you had been told he might.

Listen to Each Other. Recognize that you and your partner will not always handle the same situation in the same way. It is perfectly normal for one person to get angry about something that drives another to tears. Sometimes just listening to each other and acknowledging how the other feels can help tremendously.

You will not always have bad days on the same time schedule. This can actually be handy. Over time, some couples learn to tell instinctively when one partner is really having a bad day and the other pulls up to be supportive right then, knowing the partner will do the same for them later.

Keep in mind that you and your partner will also have differing levels of support from people outside your home, contributing to the emotional strength each has to offer in the marriage or relationship.

While it is starting to change to a more equal situation, mothers usually get more support from family, friends, coworkers, medical professionals, and others. This is partly because women are more likely to talk to others about what is happening in their lives.

It is not uncommon for a man to go to work every day and never tell anyone there about what his family is struggling with at home. Keep in mind that this way of coping is not necessarily bad. Keeping his home life a secret at work gives him a place he can go every day to focus on something besides family problems. However, it does rob him of the support he might have received from his coworkers.

Mothers also need that opportunity to take an emotional break from the pressure. Sometimes they will arrange time to read a book, take an exercise class, or do something else that allows them to take a mental break from their ongoing concerns for their child.

Spend Time Together Alone. One technique that many successful couples have used to keep their relationship strong through difficult times is setting aside a regular time for a night out. It does not have to be a fancy dinner and show; you can go for a walk in the park or around a mall, visit a library or museum, or any other activity you enjoy together. There is more about getting respite care in chapter 5 so you can make these times out possible.

Sometimes it may seem that it is impossible to get everything arranged so you two can get away together, or you decide you need some "couple" time RIGHT NOW!

Always Try to Plan Ahead. Think about what you really need to have available to take care of your relationship (and keep the elements on hand). One family was having difficulty getting help so they could leave their two young disabled children from time to time. Their answer was to have an occasional dinner night when the kids were fed their dinner and put to bed a little early. Then mom and dad would bring out the candles and a bottle of wine and have a romantic dinner at home. Those few hours of focusing on themselves as a couple strengthened them for the challenging times they knew they would continue to face ahead.

Think for a moment about what would be satisfying for you and plan to keep the things you need to make it possible on hand for when you need them. Is there a movie video that makes you both laugh? If you can afford it, would a hot tub or sauna provide the privacy and intimacy that would nourish your personal life? Use your imagination.

You might also plan to make the most of what opportunities you can carve out of your time. Small children take naps. Again, you have a short but quiet time together in your own home. If your child is in school and you are normally a homemaker, consider asking your spouse to take a vacation day from work when the two of you can enjoy those school-time hours with whatever activities best support your emotional needs.

When "For Better or Worse" Gets Worse

Remember when you and your spouse married, you planned to spend the rest of your lives together? Sometimes that commitment is tested by events that you could not have foretold when you were starting out. As you are discovering, adjusting to and learning to live with your child's disability is one of the toughest situations any person or couple can face.

You will often hear people talk about how many couples faced with the problems you are dealing with now end up divorced. What they don't talk about is how many stay together and build a stronger, more rewarding relationship as they face challenges. What do you want for yourself?

By taking care of each other and your relationship you are not only working toward the future you really want, you are giving your children the benefit of a stable, loving home to grow up in. Build on what you already have. Know that seeking the support of professionals and other parents who have lived through what you are experiencing is a sign of strength, not weakness. However, if your family unit separates, you can each still go on to build full and productive lives.

Helping Siblings Cope

It would be nice if children were just miniature adults and we could explain everything to them and have them handle their sibling's disability in a mature, rational way. However, the reality is that children are not miniature adults and they perceive things very differently from adults. Following are some guidelines for helping siblings.

Use Language Children Understand

When you talk about your disabled child to her siblings, always try to use language that they will understand at the age they are now. There will certainly be more questions as time goes on and you can give more complex answers as needed.

Listen Carefully

Pay special attention to the responses you get. Sometimes a child will feel that she somehow caused the disability. If so, assure her that you know she could not have possibly caused the medical condition her sibling is dealing with.

A sibling may also have unrealistic expectations for the future. For instance, if your child has not seen many adults with disabilities, he may assume that his sibling will outgrow her disability. As time goes on, you may want to point out adults in your community who lead active lives although they have physical disabilities. Television programs can sometimes provide role models of adults with disabilities. But too often, they hire able-bodied actors to portray characters who have disabilities. It can confuse a child to see someone acting as if he has a disability one day and the same person acting completely able-bodied in another program.

Face the Fear of Contagion

If your child's disability becomes apparent in middle or late childhood, other siblings may be afraid that they will "catch" the same thing. Normally, you can assure them that they will not have the same problems. If the disability is genetic like Duchenne muscular dystrophy, having siblings develop the condition may be a possibility your family needs to face. But there is no reason to lay this burden on younger children until necessary. Most young children will be satisfied with an answer of, "Yes, Jimmy's muscles are sick, but your's are fine right now."

If there is genetic testing for the condition in other siblings, you might want to have the tests done. If the results show that other siblings are not affected, you could decide to share that information immediately. However, if the results show that other child(ren) are going to be affected, you and your doctor should discuss when and how you will tell those children who are predisposed to the disability.

Keep the Lines of Communication Open

Talk with your children about your feelings—good and bad. When you admit that you are worried or upset, it shows them that the feelings they have are OK. Just remember not to overload them with your emotions. They are your kids, not your therapist. It is fine to say,

"I am sad that Billy's sickle cell disease makes him have days when he hurts, but I really love playing with him." A statement like that allows you to acknowledge your emotional pain, but does not make it the most important factor in your relationship with the child who is disabled.

Be Realistic

If you are facing the possible death of your child, seriously consider the siblings' age and maturity before talking to them about potential outcomes. Very young children often consider death a temporary state that people can come right back from.

Before it is time to discuss the possible death of a sibling, be sure your children understand your beliefs about spiritual matters and what happens after death, even in the simplest form. The death of a family goldfish or a character on a television show can open up the opportunity to talk about what you believe happens after death, giving your children a frame of reference for what they may experience in the future.

Try to Strike a Balance

You may be overwhelmed and exhausted by everything that is going on right now. All of your children will pick up on your verbal and nonverbal body language. Take a few moments every day just to be there for each of them. Maybe you can get a small child up a few moments early and spend that time in the rocking chair. Maybe an older child can help you fix dinner or clean up. There is something about doing dishes together that encourages shared confidences. Teens may be easier to talk to when they get in after an evening out. Sipping hot cocoa together at the kitchen table late at night seems to make it easier to open up and discuss personal feelings.

Acknowledge and Deal with Siblings' Feelings

Some, but not all, children will have times when they are embarrassed about their sibling who is disabled. Maybe they are concerned that their friends will think their sister or brother looks funny, moves funny, or uses weird equipment. This kind of talk may come out best in quiet moments when they feel they can talk to you without being judged.

Even if you don't hear them talk about being embarrassed by their sibling, their actions might tip you off. Do they bring friends home from school, or do they always find excuses why they should go over to other homes instead? Do they avoid interacting with their sibling when others are watching?

There are no easy answers for helping your children overcome their discomfort. But, there are some things that can help. You might want to be sure they really understand their sibling's disability and know the sister or brother's positive characteristics as well as the disabling conditions. If they think no one would like them because of their sibling, seeing other children get to know and accept your child with a disability may also help them get over their feelings of embarrassment.

Everyone Deserves a Childhood

A note of caution here. When one child requires a lot of personal care, it is normal to expect other family members to pitch in and help. However, you need to keep an eye on balancing the needs of different family members.

Sometimes you may suspect that your other children resent the extra work. You can't prevent them from ever feeling that way, but you can help alleviate the resentment by remembering to thank them or give them a big hug when they do something extra to help you or their sibling. You might also talk with your other children about which chores they like the best and least and arrange to rotate the least favorite chores among the group.

Finally, from time to time take an impartial look at what you expect from your children. If you find that you are beginning to ask too much of any one—or all of them—try to back off (and if necessary, find help from outside the house to fill the void). They still need time to be children and develop their own interests and talents.

Remember, You Are the Parent

When parents consistently refer to their able-bodied children as "daddy's little man" or "our family's other mother," it puts the children in the position of feeling that adult responsibilities are expected of them. Certainly they should pitch in as members of the family, but they should not carry an adult-sized load of responsibility.

Let your disabled child's siblings be as involved in the medical care as they choose to be and as can be done safely. Don't give them responsibility for life-and-death decisions, but even a responsible 10-year-old can learn to help with minor medical procedures. Some ways that siblings can help might include giving oral medications you have already measured out, assisting with braces, and plugging in electric equipment to recharge.

If your family is just finding out about the diagnosis of disability or is going through a medical crisis, you might want to let your other children's teachers, scout leaders, coaches, and other adult leaders know a little about what is going on at home. Then they can better understand changes in your children's attitude and be prepared to deal with them in a positive manner.

When one child has a medical crisis, sisters or brothers may also act out with tantrums, eating or sleeping difficulties, stomach aches, or depression. Very young children may also go back to bedwetting and loss of toilet training. Your child may want to talk with someone outside the house because of a concern about burdening you and if those adults know something about what is going on, they are more likely to be able to be supportive.

Be aware of how much attention each of your children receives from relatives and others. People will frequently bring gifts and pay special attention to the child with a disability, especially during difficult times like hospitalizations. If you find that happening, speak quietly to those people and ask them to balance their attentions. Relatives and friends are likely to be good sources of support for your nondisabled children. They may be able to give them special, individualized attention from time to time when you have to deal with heavy responsibilities for your child with a disability. They can also give support in more subtle ways, like showing up for the baseball and soccer games your able-bodied children play, going to Scouting award ceremonies where one of the children is being recognized, and other special occasions and everyday events.

Recognize Each Family Member's Strengths and Needs

On a day-to-day basis, you also will want to be aware of the ways you recognize accomplishments by different members of the family. It is very easy to slip into a pattern where you enthusiastically praise and reward any accomplishment by your child with a disability, yet accept the accomplishments of your able-bodied child as normal and not needing special recognition. All children need and deserve recognition for what they achieve. Try to keep a balance in the family so no child feels taken for granted.

If you are in public and a stranger approaches and says something like, "What a sweet child," to your child with a disability, in front of your other children, it never hurts to respond, "I think all my children are sweet," especially if you think your other children are listening. It is much more important that you work toward building your children into a cohesive group, all of whom will feel they are important to their parents, than affirming the stranger's comments, which suggest that one of your children is more important than the others.

Two very real concerns that you seriously need to watch for are:

The guilty child. Earlier you read about the fact that children often think they have done something that brought the disability to their sibling. The guilt they feel is very real to them. It is especially touching because there is almost always nothing that they could have done to change the disabled child's condition. If your assurances are not enough to help your able-bodied children move past the feelings of guilt, you might want to find a peer support group or counselor who can help them deal with their feelings and move on.

The perfect child. This may not seem like a problem at all—at first. Occasionally, children will attempt to compensate for their sibling with a disability by being perfect children. They try to be the most obedient, the most helpful, the best students, the most outstanding athletes, or all of the above.

If you suspect that a child is somehow trying to be perfect to compensate for a sibling's disability, you may need to spend some extra time with that child. Certainly, having a sibling with a disability has inspired some young people to work toward remarkable goals. There is nothing wrong with having children excel at whatever they try—as long as they do all that work for themselves, not because they feel responsible to have an impact in the world for themselves and their sibling.

Siblings Need Special Support

If you suspect your nondisabled children could use some extra support, you have a number of options available to you.

Talk with Your Children. Do they just need more personal attention or are they really looking for someone to talk to about what is going on?

If they need more personal attention, you can work with family members and others who see your children regularly (babysitters, teachers, Sunday school teachers, scout leaders, and athletic coaches, for example) to be sure your children are getting the support and recognition they need.

If your children are looking for someone to talk to, you have a number of options. Do not be upset if they want someone outside the immediate family to talk with. They may feel that sharing all their feelings with you will be a burden to you. There are a number of safe outlets you can find for them to talk about their feelings.

Make it possible for them to talk with their pediatrician or your disabled child's primary physician. They may have some negative assumptions about the disability their sister or brother has that the doctor can help them overcome.

Make Sure Important Adults in Their Lives Know of Your Concerns (and are knowledgeable about your other child's disability). Sometimes hearing someone else, such as a teacher or school counselor, say the very thing you have been saying helps children accept the truth.

Search for Youth Support Groups. Consider checking with your doctors, social workers, disability organizations, and schools to find out if there are any peer support groups for siblings of children who have disabilities. Just like adults, kids are often relieved to find that the feelings that scare them so much are also felt by others. Peer support has the added advantage of allowing them to talk about their experiences and feelings that they suspect might sound cruel or selfish to people who have never lived in their situation.

Be Willing to Consider Professional Help. If you have made your best effort and you feel that one or more of your children are not handling the emotional burden of having a disabled sibling in a healthy way, consider looking for a therapist to help them deal with their feelings. You might start by asking at disability-related organizations about therapists who have successfully worked with siblings.

Keep It All in Perspective. While your child's disability certainly adds a layer of complexity to the family situation, no child reaches adulthood without having to deal with some difficult situations. In all likelihood, you will find that all of your children will have times when they find life challenging—whether the kids are disabled or not. Don't expect to be able to smooth every rough time. It would not be healthy for any of you. Your job is to be there to support your children as they learn to deal with life, so they can become emotionally healthy adults. No one ever said it would be easy, but be sure you don't miss the good times along the way.

One saying that has helped countless parents get through countless bad days is, "The child who seems most unlovable is the one who needs love the most." When a child becomes especially difficult, try to respond with love. Then, if you need to express your anger or frustration at that child or situation, go ventilate to someone in your support network to help you get your balance back.

Concerns for the Future

At some point in time, especially in the teen years, your able-bodied children may start to ask whether they will be responsible for the sibling who is disabled when you get old or die.

Certainly a lot of factors will go into your expectations of what kind of family relationship you expect your children to have with each other as adults. In terms of who takes responsibility for whom, the ability of the sibling with a disability to become self-supporting and live independently will determine whether anyone needs to consider being responsible for another at all.

If you do have an expectation that one child will need extra assistance as an adult, you may want to talk with the others (when they are old enough to really understand). Explain not only what your expectations are, but also what resources you expect to have available for them so they do not feel the full weight of responsibility falling on their young shoulders.

You do not have to be terribly explicit to your teens, but you might note any relatives who will be able to help, plans for the future you have already set in motion, the kinds of social service programs you expect your children to be able to access, and whether you expect to leave financial resources to cover expenses. Older teens and young adults may ask for more detailed information. On the positive side, the changes in the law and social attitudes in recent years have created new opportunities for people with disabilities to become self-supporting and lead independent lives. In all likelihood, that is the future your child with a disability can look forward to.

Your teens (able-bodied and disabled) will also reach a time when they begin to wonder if the children they might have someday could have the same disability. If there is a genetic component to your child's disability, you will want to have the most up-to-date information to share with them. Even if you had genetic counseling during your child's diagnostic process, if a few years or more pass before your teens ask about their risk, consider making another appointment for genetic counseling and taking your teens along.

Medical research is moving along at a phenomenal rate, and the ability of doctors to identify people at risk for genetic conditions improves every day. That means that their ability to assure some people that they are not at risk for passing on genetic conditions is improving, too.

If you would like to read more about how other families whose children have physical and/or mental disabilities have dealt with sibling issues, try *It Isn't Fair! Siblings of Children with Disabilities,* which was edited by Stanley D. Klein and Maxwell J. Schleifer, published by Bergin & Garvey. ($14.95 plus shipping & handling. Call (800)535–1910 to order.)

Special Handling of Grandparents

Handling your child's grandparents can present a special challenge and hopefully a special support.

In some ways it may be harder for them to accept your child's disability than it is even for you. Grandparents have hopes and dreams for the child, just as you do. In addition, when things start to go wrong, they not only hurt for the grandchild, they hurt for you, their child. Your parents also may not realize that while you are dealing with your own emotions about the disability, you may also be feeling grief over not being able to give them the grandchild of their dreams.

Sometimes, their grief makes it difficult for them to be supportive, especially in the beginning. Occasionally, old family conflicts will flare up at this time and you and your spouse may find yourselves listening to old complaints about why you should never have married in the first place. Sometimes, especially if they are not able to see the child frequently, grandparents refuse to believe anything is really wrong, or cling to the belief that the child simply will outgrow the disability.

Fortunately, many times grandparents become a tremendous source of strength and support for young families, either right away or over time. They bring their love, energy, and practical help (and sometimes their checkbook) to help smooth the way.

The Grandparent's Role

What should you insist on from your child's grandparents?

That They Respect Your Marriage and Family. While they can certainly advise you, the medical and lifestyle decisions that will have to be made now and in the future are yours—not theirs. It also does no good to try to assign blame, as in, "If it's genetic, it must have come from his side of the family." Remind them (firmly, if necessary) that what your child needs now is for everyone to focus on the present and future.

That They Learn About Their Grandchild's Disability. This is especially useful to help them come to grips with the situation. If they are far away, send them literature and possibly put them in touch with their local office of organizations that focus on your child's disability. They might call and see if there are other grandparents in their area who they can talk with about their concerns.

If the grandparents live nearby, be sure they have a chance to see your child frequently. Consider bringing them along to some medical appointments so they can meet your child's care providers and have a chance to ask any questions they might have.

That They Treat This Grandchild as They Do Their Others. Certainly some accommodations may have to be made over time to deal with the disability (especially accessibility at their home). However, grandparents should not spoil this child more than the others, or treat him as less lovable or desirable just because of the disability. Either behavior will have negative repercussions throughout the family for years to come.

That They Check with You Before Doing Something They Assume Will Be Helpful. Raising a child who has a disability is going to be different in many ways from the family your parents raised. Grandparents need to respect those differences and how they affect your needs. After all, you are managing medical, psychological, and social situations that they never had to face.

An example might be a grandparent who wants to start a trust fund for the disabled child. However, if your child is qualified for free medical care through a government program, all the assets he acquires may have to be spent before the program will pick up any bills. There are ways to arrange financial trusts, but they must be handled carefully by experienced professional attorneys and accountants.

That They Give Unconditional Love. The best gift grandparents can give your child is their unconditional love, even if they are unable to assist you in any other way. On the other hand, if do they offer to help, take them at their word.

Accept Their Offers for Help

You already know the experiences and skills your parents have. What specific things can they do that would be useful to you and your family? Maybe you need simple things like hot meals prepared or errands run. Maybe you need help searching out support groups, following up with insurance companies, or other time-consuming activities.

Not every child has grandparents and, occasionally, no matter how hard parents work to build a good relationship, the grandparents are not really "there" for the family. Yet every child deserves the special kind of love that grandparents can give.

If necessary, feel free to search out grandparent-substitutes. These could be people you already know from your neighborhood, job, or church. You might also check with your librarian or local volunteer agency about foster-grandparenting groups. These people may offer a friendly ear or a shoulder to cry on for you, and their unconditional love will be a tremendous gift to your child.

Extended Family—Special Questions/Special Help

Relating to your extended family adds yet another layer of complication and support.

Brothers and Sisters

Do you and your spouse have sisters and brothers? If so, hopefully they will become an important part of your personal support network. They can be emotionally and physically supportive from the start and for years to come. Keep in mind that your siblings often have some unique concerns that they may be reluctant to bring up, at least in the beginning.

It is very normal for your grown brothers and sisters to want specific information about your child's disability—and what caused it. They may be frightened that their children could potentially face the same problem in the future.

By the time you have a diagnosis for your child, you have probably already asked the medical team about the genetics of the condition, the possibility of it occurring in a subsequent pregnancy, and prenatal tests that are currently available. Share that information with your siblings, even if they have not asked yet. They have undoubtedly been thinking about it.

When there is a genetic aspect to your child's disability (and especially if there are tests to identify carriers), ask your physicians for names and programs you can refer your family members to for testing wherever they live.

You must also develop a strategy for handling the concerns of your sibling's children—your child's cousins. Sometimes the fact that a cousin looks different, acts different, or has strange equipment can puzzle youngsters. They may be especially concerned about whether they can "catch" it.

Be ready to talk with your siblings about ways they can explain your child's disability to their children in terms that are easily understood. Be available to answer more questions when they come up, especially as the children grow and are ready for more sophisticated answers. Also, be certain you tell them that they cannot "catch" it like a cold and it's OK to play together. Over the years to come, the cousins are likely to become an important source of camaraderie and support for your child if you help get the relationship off to a good start.

Include Your Aunts and Uncles in Your Support Network

Experiences with your own aunts and uncles may have some of the same benefits and drawbacks as the relationship with your parents. They care about you and your child and may be very willing to help. Plan to educate them as you do your parents. If the information chain in your family goes through your parents to their other relatives, you might want to take a moment when you see the others to be sure the information is getting through accurately.

Your Grandparents

If you are fortunate enough to still have your own grandparents in your life, they, too, will have an important role in your support network. You will need to be sensitive to their physical and emotional status when you decide exactly how much information to give them and how much help to expect from them. It is very possible to become a great-grandparent before you are old enough to retire, but, on the other hand, your grandparents could be quite old and facing debilitating problems of their own.

If your grandparents still enjoy a vigorous, active lifestyle, they may be able to offer you the same types of support that your parents do. Accept their help when you need it. No one likes to feel that they are no longer useful just because they have accumulated a lot of years.

Whether your grandparents are able to provide physical assistance or not, you are likely to find that their maturity will enable them to be a source of emotional support and wisdom for you and your family.

Other Family Members

Your family may very well include some variations not mentioned here. Families can include "blends" from previous marriages and even close friends who become honorary family members. Only you can decide how much you want to have to do with any member of your extended family. Most of them will probably want to be loving and helpful to you now and in the future.

Stay Focused on Your Child's Needs

If any family members or friends try to make you to do something with, or for, your child that you are not comfortable with, remember that your primary responsibility is to take care of your child. Don't let *anyone* push you into looking for yet another doctor who will give a more acceptable diagnosis, trying an untested treatment, fighting the school district, or filing a lawsuit unless it is really what you want to do.

In the end, you and your child are the ones who will bear the burden for the paths you follow. Don't allow the "shoulds" that other people try to put on you to keep you from having the time and resources to do what you really feel is important.

Your families can be a great blessing to you and your child. Remember that you are an adult now and have every right to make decisions for yourself and your child. No family is perfect, even on television.

Give family members the information they need, be firm about your decisions, be gracious when they are helpful, and they will probably be there for you for a lifetime.

4

Should You Consult a Psychological Therapist?

When to Look for a Therapist

There are times when you should consider talking with a professional psychological therapist yourself or taking your child to visit one. Certainly, if you or someone in your family is talking about or threatening suicide you *must* take the situation seriously and get professional help. In an emergency, your phone directory, directory assistance operator, or police emergency number can refer you to crisis help.

On the other hand, many people go through difficult life experiences without seeking or needing therapy. Often they find emotional resources within themselves, find strength through their spiritual faith, develop a network of family and/or friends who can provide emotional support, seek out other parents who can offer mutual support, and/or find professional help through nonclinical professionals such as pastors, priests, or rabbis.

A caution here. Sometimes people will assume that just because you are dealing with a difficult situation when your child has a disability, you should be in therapy. If you are coping well and know you are, it can be irritating. If you are coping, but having problems, it can make you doubt yourself. If you know you are having serious problems, you have probably already been thinking about therapy.

In most circumstances, you should be the one who decides whether you will pursue professional counseling. A notable exception would be if you find yourself developing a dependence on a chemical substance (like alcohol) and friends or family suggest that you seek treatment. Consider whether they might be right.

There are some other signs that you need help. If you find yourself desiring significantly more or less sleep than normal, losing interest in eating, unable to make decisions that used to come without stress, or feeling so depressed that it interferes with your regular life for weeks or months, you may want to consider ways to help you move on with your life.

Some people find that they are able to manage their problems when they accept peer support from other parents whose children are disabled, work with their spouse/partner to develop a stronger relationship, nurture themselves by acknowledging their feelings and finding personal satisfaction in other parts of their lives that help them cope (such as work or exercise), or seek psychological support from medical professionals or therapists. Each person must decide what kind of support he or she needs to be able to handle his or her life satisfactorily.

Types of Therapy

If you decide to work with a professional therapist, you owe it to yourself to be a good consumer. The professional you engage will be working with you on a very personal level to help you reach your therapeutic goals.

According to the American Psychological Association (APA), one of the issues you should consider before engaging a therapist is his or her therapeutic orientation (or way of viewing problem solving).

You will find that most therapists do not follow a specific school of thought, but combine features from different types of therapy depending on the kinds of problems each client is dealing with. However, some therapists focus primarily on one specific approach. It is important that you understand what techniques a therapist prefers before you choose the therapist who you want to work with.

Some of the formal techniques therapists choose (and each may have its own subcategories) include:

Behavioral. Primarily geared toward removing symptoms such as potentially self-destructive behavior patterns. Usually this type of therapy is short term.

Psychodynamic. This longer term therapy takes a historical point of view to the client's past in order to discover the reasons behind behavior, conflicts, and unconscious motivations. One type of psychodynamic therapy is psychoanalysis, which tends to be long term and require four to five visits per week.

Group therapy. Led by a trained therapist, this type of therapy is especially appropriate for people who are having interpersonal problems. There are often specialized groups for people who have similar issues to deal with. Group therapy is usually less expensive than individual therapy.

Cognitive. This therapy technique seeks to correct negative thinking patterns. It is very interactive.

Interpersonal therapy. Focusing on the client's interpersonal relationships, this therapy technique works to relate relationships and the other problems and issues in the client's life.

Finding a Therapist

When you decide to seek a therapist, there are many resources you can contact for a referral. Plan to make a call and even set up brief introductory meetings with several prospective therapists either by phone or in person. Ask them about the therapeutic techniques they prefer to use and the way they prefer to deal with clients.

The two main types of professionals are psychologists and psychiatrists.

Psychologists must be licensed by the state in which they practice. Although requirements for licensure vary from state to state, most require a doctoral degree (Ph.D., Psy.D., or Ed.D.) as a minimum. With a strong background in assessment, psychologist are qualified to diagnose and treat many disorders. Psychologists who demonstrate advanced levels of competence can be awarded Board Certification by the American Board of Professional Psychology.

Psychiatrists are M.D.s or D.O.s and their training is primarily focused on the biological aspects of mental illness. Since they are physicians, they can prescribe medications to be used in conjunction with treatment of mental disorders.

Psychiatrists often refer patients to psychologists and vice versa depending on the therapeutic needs of the individual client.

Depending on your needs and the professionals available locally, you also may be referred to a psychiatric social worker (who probably practices through a hospital or clinic). These professionals are certified and, in some cases, licensed in the state where they practice. They are trained to help you cope with day-to-day problems, not to treat serious disorders.

Looking for Help in All the Right Places

Some people you might want to contact for referrals to a therapist include:

- A friend or family member who has benefited from therapy.
- Other families you know who are dealing with the same diagnosis and who have benefited from therapy.
- Your child's physician (or yours).
- Your spiritual counselor (especially if you are looking for assistance with behavior-oriented problems rather than spiritually oriented problems).
- Professionals you are already dealing with, such as social workers, school guidance counselors, psychologists, and so on.
- Patient-services professionals at social service or disability-related organizations you are already in contact with. They may be in a very good position to refer you to professionals who are experienced in dealing with families who are experiencing the same problems you are facing.

Questions to Ask a Therapist

Like any professional you are considering hiring—from the mechanic who works on your car to the neurologist you consult on your child's medical condition—you should ask questions to determine whether your needs and goals are compatible with the services the therapist has to offer.

Some of those questions should include:

- How do you see the problems I am struggling with?
- What form of therapy do you use?
- How will we work together to solve my problems?
- What is your experience in dealing with disability issues?
- How long do you think it will take?
- What is your licensure/certification?
- What is your educational background?
- How frequently do you suggest we have sessions?
- How much will the therapy cost? What is the rate per session? Is there a sliding scale or will it be covered by my insurance? Will you help me work out a payment plan?

After you have interviewed a therapist, there are some questions you should ask yourself, including:

- Can I trust this person?
- Do I feel comfortable sharing things with him or her?
- Is this person really listening to my problems?
- Does this person have a sense of me as an individual?
- Am I being understood?
- Am I comfortable that this person will give me advice that will work for me?
- Is this therapist a good match for me (and possibly my family)?

Are You Satisfied?

Most people would be suspicious of someone who promises to fix all their problems right away. Rightly so. Sometimes therapy takes months or years; at other times, a therapist really can point out ways to make your relationships work better with only a few meet-ings.

Once you have decided to work with a particular therapist, you may need to allow some time to work out the bugs in the relationship. However, if after about six visits you do not feel that you are making progress, it may be time to consider changing therapists. This does not mean that either you or the therapist have failed. The therapist/ client relationship is a very intense, personal relationship and it may take several tries to find just the right fit. As the APA says, therapy is not something that is done *to* you; it is something that is done *with* you.

In the end, *only you* can decide whether you would benefit from therapy. Don't let anyone else drive you to it if you don't think you need it, and don't let anyone else keep you from it if you think you need this help. You are the only one who can decide what you really need.

5

Building Your Medical Team

The Importance of Teamwork

Have you ever seen a boating event called crew racing? A group of people in a long boat rows smoothly and in unison to reach its goal. Can you imagine what it would be like if the rowers decided to head in different directions and row at their own pace? They would never get anywhere.

You need to assemble a medical team that will work together like a winning crew team. You are the captain of that team—the person who is responsible for making sure the team you build can meet your child's needs and yours. (Don't neglect the fact that you have needs, especially for accurate information explained in a way you can understand and training in any medical techniques you will be expected to perform for your child.)

The most crucial member of your team is the primary physician. This doctor coordinates all the phases of your child's medical care. Whenever you see other health professionals, they should send a written report of the appointment and their findings back to your child's primary physician.

This is important because sometimes specialists tend to see your child only in terms of their specialty. Your primary physician can put the opinions and advice in perspective in light of your child's overall needs.

Parents whose child has a relatively involved disability often will tell of the frustration of seeing a number of medical advisors for different aspects of their child's problem—and each professional recommends a specific therapy or activity the parent should do "for only 20 minutes, three times a day." The parents know all the advice is good, but there simply are not enough hours in the day. This is one of the many times when your primary physician can help you sift through the options and choose those that are the best and most effective.

Your child's primary physician is normally your family practitioner or pediatrician since this person also can take care of routine immunizations and occasional illnesses. In some cases, this person may be a specialist in some phase of your child's health who you have to see very frequently if the disability is very complicated.

How to Choose a Physician

Aside from the obvious need to choose an excellent physician, there are two other qualifications you should keep in mind.

First, does he or she have some enthusiasm for handling a complicated case? Managing a patient with complex medical needs and integrating other professionals in the care of that patient is time consuming and demanding. You want someone who sees this in a positive light rather than as a burden.

Second, does he or she respond to your needs in a timely fashion? Over the years you are likely to need a number of referrals to different medical specialists and quite a few letters written to school personnel and government programs. Is this physician likely to be able to send these letters out when you need them?

There are some other indicators you should consider because they can help you determine how successful your relationship with this physician is likely to be. When you visit a new doctor's office look around and ask yourself:

- Is the office "child friendly?" Are there toys to play with and are delicate or potentially dangerous pieces of medical equipment safely out of reach?
- Does the staff make you and your child feel welcome?

- Do they make your child as comfortable as possible in the office during exams and necessary procedures?
- Are staff members willing to take your child from the office and care for him while you talk with the doctor?

Filling Out Your Team

Once you have chosen your primary physician, you can work with this person to develop the rest of your team. Depending on your child's individual needs, you may find yourself adding different medical specialists, physical and/or occupational therapists, dentists and/or orthodontists, respite nurses, visiting nurses, orthotists, equipment suppliers, equipment repair shops, and others.

Guidelines for Choosing Health Professionals

How do you find the right doctors and other medical professionals for your child and family? Although it is fairly simple, it is usually somewhat time consuming.

You want to find someone who you and your child are comfortable with—someone who is competent to provide the services you expect and who is comfortable working as part of your medical team and personal network.

What kinds of specialists will you need? In Appendix I there is a listing of the common types of specialists families see. Your child's individual situation will determine which of these medical specialists you will need to consult.

Places to Look for Medical Professionals

Referral from Your Current Provider. This works even in the earliest stages, especially if you are looking for specialists. For instance, you may ask your childbirth instructor or obstetrician about pediatricians who have worked well with other families dealing with disabilities.

Referral from Organizations Dealing with Similar Conditions. When you contact a diagnosis-specific organization (such as the Arthritis

Foundation or United Cerebral Palsy Association) or a more general disability-related organization (such as the Easter Seal Society), you will find that there are physicians who work with the organization and have an interest in serving children with problems similar to your child's.

Referrals from Other Parents Who Have Children with Disabilities. These referrals are especially helpful in two ways. First, they can help you find dentists and other professionals you may need for reasons unrelated to your child's disability, but who are already working successfully with children like yours. Second, other parents are somewhat more likely than other professionals to share with you the negative as well as positive traits of a professional.

Referrals from Other Specialists You Already Deal with and Whose Opinion You Respect. These referrals are likely to have a strong team-building element since in all likelihood the specialist already knows he works well with the person he is recommending.

Referral from Medical Schools in Your Area. Even if your child is not yet diagnosed, you can start with what you suspect. Is your child moving differently from other's his age? If so, you may want to contact the neurology department. Are you concerned that he is not hearing you? Then you will want to ask for a referral to an audiologist or otorhinolaryngologist (ear, nose, and throat specialist).

Other Options

Another way to gather information is to pursue the internationally recognized experts by going to conferences or reading articles in medical journals. These journals are available in medical school libraries. As a parent, you can read materials at the library or photocopy them, but you probably will not be permitted to check them out. You also can contact the authors of articles you found most interesting to ask about their current research projects or other research projects they are aware of.

Margaret, a parent whose child had a chromosomal abnormality that resulted in a physical disability, was devastated by this diagnosis. She was especially concerned because the diagnosing physician had given her a long list of complications that can occur with this diagnosis. She searched out articles about her child's condition, found out that the National Institutes of Health (NIH) was a resource for information and called. When NIH told her that there would be a major medical conference on the diagnosis her child had in only two days, Margaret decided to drop everything and go.

The first year she attended the conference, the clinical nature of the event focused on the more complicated cases and was very frightening. The next year, Margaret went to the same conference and met the one doctor who made all her efforts to find information about her child's diagnosis worthwhile. He must have noticed that her interest was more than professional, so he came up to talk with her. When she admitted her fears, he asked, "Didn't anyone ever tell you that if your child wasn't born with those complications that she will never develop them?" In that instant, she was relieved of her greatest fears and was free to start coping with the situation the way it really was.

Places to Look for Information

You may not have the time, resources, or interest in going to medical conferences in order to get the most up-to-date information about your child's diagnosis. However, you can educate yourself and stay informed by working closely with the medical experts in your child's condition and getting on the mailing lists to receive newsletters from organizations that specialize in your child's diagnosis or similar conditions. You also can do an independent survey of the literature either through computer database searches or by spending time in your local medical school library.

How to Build a Good Relationship with Your Child's Doctor and Other Medical Professionals

Ask Questions

No one becomes an expert overnight. You will need to learn a whole new vocabulary. If you do not understand a word someone uses, ask what it means and write it down so you won't forget. You most likely will have to learn about treatment techniques or medications you never heard of before. Be sure you understand them before you try to implement them. You will also find yourself with other questions about things you never thought about before. Don't be embarrassed if, at first, you are not as knowledgeable about your child's medical condition as you would like to be. The important thing is to learn as much as you can in order to be the best possible parent and advocate for your child. Good medical professionals will work with you to help you gain a full understanding of your child's condition.

Keep Good Records

It is very important to keep a list of your child's medications (and his reactions to each one). Other records should include letters and evaluations that professionals have written at different times for medical referrals, school district records, and evaluations or records from organizations you receive respite from. Take a notebook to all medical appointments so you can record the recommendations you receive, directions for administering medications, instructions for therapies to be done at home, and other important information.

Getting to Know You . . .

Once you have identified a professional you are considering using, make an appointment to talk with him or her. Bring a list of the questions you want to ask and some paper to take notes (this is a good time to start that notebook, or ask permission to bring a small tape recorder) so you can review the information you get at home. The emotional impact of a first meeting can make it difficult to recall what was said later.

Also, consider taking along your spouse, a grandparent, or a friend whose opinion you value and who will not try to dominate the meeting. Afterwards, that person can serve as a good sounding board.

Expect to spend time talking about your child (including her social and psychological development), her medical history, and her current condition and symptoms as you see them. *Be honest.* If you have certain expectations from this physician, now is the time to voice them.

If your child's condition is life-threatening or likely to become so, you *must* talk to the physician about how aggressive you think medical treatment should be. There are no right or wrong answers. Some families decide they want to let nature take its course. Other families in the same situation want to treat aggressively as long as there is hope that their child will return to a satisfying lifestyle. Still others choose to treat aggressively until the last possible moment.

On another level, some families want the best possible outcome at any cost whether it is in terms of surgical procedures, orthopedic correction, orthodontic treatment, and so on. Others decide that pursuing the optimum medical outcome in a particular situation will incur other costs they are not willing to accept in terms of pain, loss of school time, or financial expense.

It is very important that your physician understand your views and be willing to work with you in terms of your family's values. At the same time, remember that physicians are people too. They bring their own experience and values to their professional lives. If you feel that you and this particular physician are not going to be able to work together, you should look for someone else.

Questions for the Doctor

Here are some of the kinds of questions you should ask:

- How does his training and experience prepare him to work with someone with your child's medical problems?
- How many patients does he have (or has he had) with similar problems?
- Is he affiliated with any organizations dealing with your child's specific problem?
- Is he affiliated with a medical school? Physicians who are affiliated with medical schools are more likely to be involved with the latest research and treatments.

- At what hospitals does he have admitting privileges? Do any of those hospitals have specific programs for families dealing with similar problems?

- If you are dealing with a health maintenance organization (HMO), is this the facility most patients with similar diagnoses are referred to for treatment in your region?

- How much are his fees? Is there anyone in his office who can help you deal with insurance companies and access government programs?

- What he would do and where he would go if this were his child?

Remember, just because you talk with a physician, you are not making a commitment to use his services. A bad match of family and physician will only result in a continuing struggle that will make everything you have to deal with more difficult. When you find the right physicians, they are worth their weight in gold.

When to Fire Health Professionals

The Right Reasons

There may come a time when you need or want to change to a different physician, therapist, or other health professional. Following are some key indicators to help you recognize those times.

A Poor Working Relationship. There can be a wide variety of reasons for this. Sometimes you or your child may not feel comfortable (or feel that the professional is not comfortable with you).

Communication Problems. Occasionally, you may feel the professional is patronizing you when you prefer to be treated like a team member.

Philosophical Differences. Medical professionals are people too and have their own beliefs, just as you do. If you feel that the professional's personal philosophy is contrary to your family's treatment goals, you may be more comfortable working with someone else.

Lack of Competence in Your Child's Condition. No one is an expert at everything, and even specialists may focus on one area of their specialty above another. In the rare situation where you suspect the professional is truly incompetent, consider contacting his or her hospital administrator or other superior and/or the state licensing agency with your concerns.

Lack of Availability. It is unrealistic to expect medical professionals to be available to you constantly. However, if your child's problem is such that you need to be able to get help quickly and the professional you deal with frequently cannot be reached or does not have anyone covering for him, this could be a problem. In this situation, you might consider choosing a professional in a group setting where there are others to cover for him.

Changes in Your Child's Preference. This is an iffy reason to change, especially if you have a good, long-term relationship with the professional. However, the time may come when you should consider it. For instance, when your child hits puberty, he or she may want to change to a physician of the same sex to be more comfortable during exams and when asking personal questions. While there is absolutely no reason why a different-sex physician could not handle all this perfectly well, talk with the doctor about the situation. He or she may be able to help you to either alleviate your child's concerns or find another physician.

Acting on Her Beliefs

By the time he was nine months old, it became apparent to a mother in the Southeast that her son's physical development was not normal. Gloria began taking him to a neurologist who referred to herself as a developmental therapist. For a while, things went OK, although she was not completely satisfied with the doctor's attitude. Then the doctor started pushing her to allow experimental drug therapies on her son. When the doctor could not give Gloria information she wanted about potential side effects, she said no.

Then the doctor began berating Gloria for not agreeing to the experimental treatment. It was time to make a change. Gloria calmly

(Continued)

(Continued)
told the doctor that they would not be returning and left. Now the son is being treated by a physician whose philosophy is closer to Gloria's.

This situation was certainly more dramatic than most times when a family chooses to change physicians. Remember, you have the right to change doctors any time you feel the relationship is no longer beneficial. However, you should think carefully before you take that step.

The Wrong Reasons

At some time, you might find yourself considering changing medical professionals for reasons that are inappropriate—not that you don't have the absolute right to change professionals. It is just that, at times, the emotional impact of what you are living through can cloud your ability to analyze a situation rationally. For instance:

You dislike the diagnosis. Changing doctors is not likely to change the diagnosis. However, it is very reasonable to ask for a referral for a second opinion (see chapter 2). Most professionals would consider your request very normal. If the physician acts threatened or becomes abusive when you ask for a referral, these are excellent reasons for finding another professional.

Your child wasn't cured. Some things simply cannot be cured. If you have any doubts or questions that your current professional is not answering to your satisfaction, get a second opinion (see chapter 2). Changing physicians is not likely to change your child's diagnosis and may delay whatever treatments or progress that can be made while you find a new professional and bring her up to speed on your child's problem.

Pressure from others. You may experience pressure from family or friends who want you to use the professional of their choice. Choosing a health professional is a matter of personal preference—yours and your child's. If the professional they are urging you to use is highly respected in his field, you might ask your physician if the other doctor would be suitable to use for a second opinion, if you want or need one.

Tips on Changing Professionals

When you decide to change professionals, you can locate new ones to interview using the techniques given on pages 51 and 52.

If your medical insurance is with a health maintenance organization (HMO) or preferred provider organization (PPO), you may need to choose a different professional within the organization so your appointments will be covered. In this case, the organization may have staff people with titles such as "advice nurse" who you can contact for information about which professionals are most likely to meet your family's particular needs.

When you make an appointment with a potential new medical professional, make sure you know what is needed in terms of medical records and how that is normally handled in the office or organization. If you are going from one private practitioner to another, you may need to write a letter asking the first practitioner to send copies of the records. If you are dealing within an HMO, the records should already be available to both practitioners.

If your relationship with the professional you are leaving remains civil or cordial, it is a nice touch to drop her a note thanking her for the help she has given you after you have chosen your new health care provider.

Paying the Bills

As you develop your medical team, don't be shy about asking the professionals you work with:

- What is your fee schedule?

- How will your office work with our insurance carrier?

- How do you handle fees that may not be covered by our insurance plan?

- Will you work with us to arrange a payment plan if necessary?

- Can you put us in touch with any programs that may cover some or all of the cost of our child's treatment?

Beyond Insurance

Frequently, families find that the costs associated with handling their child's disability outstrip their insurance or their ability to pay. When that happens, there are other organizations you can look to for help. Three resources you should consider are the Shriners Hospitals, public health clinics, and disability-specific organizations that may offer clinics or assistance with equipment purchases.

The Shriners Hospitals. For more than 70 years, the Shrine of North America has been known for its generous network of specialized hospitals that treat children who have serious burns or crippling conditions including spinal cord injuries.

Children from infancy to their 18th birthday are admitted to Shriners for in- or out-patient treatment if, in the opinion of the hospital's chief of staff, there is a reasonable possibility that treatment will benefit the child and if treatment at another facility would place a financial burden on the patient's family or guardian. The free services include all in-patient and out-patient care, diagnostic services, surgery, medical care, casts, braces, X rays, rehabilitation programs, recreation, clothing, and continuation of the child's education.

In addition to the patient services they provide, Shriners Hospitals conduct major medical research programs into a variety of crippling diseases (such as brittle bone disease or juvenile rheumatoid arthritis) and the treatment of burn injuries (the metabolic and nutritional aspects of severe burns, limitation of scarring through surgical treatment, and better wound healing).

The Shriners never send a bill to the families and do not use any government funds or insurance monies. They raise funds to cover the expenses by holding local and national events throughout the year, including their famous circus. They also organize the East-West Shrine Classic football game in Palo Alto, California, every year—the oldest all-star college football game in existence.

One factor that makes the benefits of being a Shriners patient stand out is the way they go beyond just helping your child function to really helping him reach his dreams.

Running After a Dream

Tony Volpentest (his real name) was born without hands or feet and doctors told his family that he would never walk without prostheses. Fortunately, Tony was too young to understand them and he did learn to balance and walk on the ends of his legs.

As he grew, Tony demonstrated a real flare for athletics and a willingness to work hard that is the hallmark of a champion. Surprisingly, he found he had a special gift for sprinting, even without feet. However, as he became more and more competitive, he realized that he needed special foot orthotics to become the fastest racer he was capable of being.

This is where the Shriners Hospital came in. Tony was already a patient and the staff was familiar with his disability and his urge to compete. Together, Tony and the staff worked to build him a state-of-the-art set of feet especially designed for racing.

Tony's ultimate racing goal was to represent the United States in the Paralympics in Barcelona in 1992. The Paralympics were scheduled after the Summer Olympics and were for athletes from around the world who have physical disabilities. After years of hard work, Tony achieved his dream and was chosen for the team to run both the 100-meter and 200-meter sprints.

Facing the very best amputee runners in the world and in front of a cheering audience of 55,000 (including the King and Queen of Spain), Tony sprinted to the head of the pack and won both of his races. In addition to becoming a champion, his wins earned him the title of "Fastest Leg Amputee Sprinter in the World."

Certainly, Tony was born to be a winner and he has earned his honors through his dedication and hard work. Yet, at the same time, the Shriners Hospital shares in his victories because of the extra mile they went to make sure he had the best possible equipment.

Does your child have a dream that cannot be achieved without special medical help or equipment? If you think your child may qualify for help through the Shriners, call them at (800) 237-5055 in the United States or (800) 361-7256 in Canada.

Public Health Clinics. Some families use a clinic or public health facility as the primary medical provider for their child. The medical professionals at these clinics can refer you to specialists or clinics where your child can get the specific care he needs. There may be a charge based on a sliding scale depending on your family income. In other cases, the costs may be fully covered by government programs.

If your child is already covered under Medicaid, WICC (Women, Infants, and Children's Care), or local health department and/or Department of Health programs in your state, you should contact your case worker for more information about how to access the programs and services your child needs. If you are not currently involved in one of these programs, but have a low income, you may qualify for assistance.

Eligibility is determined by your state program of public assistance on the basis of broad federal guidelines. There are differences between eligibility requirements and types of services you may qualify for based on where you live. Usually, you will be eligible for Medicaid if you are receiving welfare or other public assistance benefits, Supplemental Security Income, or are disabled. Even if you suspect that your income is too high to qualify, your child may be eligible if his medical expenses exceed a given percentage of your household's annual income.

You can get more information on Medicaid by calling your local or state welfare office or writing to:

Health Care Financing Administration
Inquiries Staff
Room GF-3, East Lowrise Building
Baltimore, MD 21207

Disability-Specific Organizations. Once you have an idea of the type of disability your child has, you should contact organizations that specialize in similar conditions. Many of them offer assistance in the medical arena. Some examples include:

- Free clinics (and limited equipment purchases) through the Muscular Dystrophy Association for patients who have neuromuscular conditions.

▪ Funding through the Billy Barty Foundation for families whose children have dwarfism. This funding can assist with transportation to specialized clinics at certain hospitals and lodging for parents when a child is in the hospital.

There is a listing of disability-specific organizations in Appendix 2.

These are only three options you can pursue when you need help paying for your child's medical needs. There may be other programs that are available in your state or community. You can ask social workers you meet through hospitalizations or disability related organizations about resources that may be available where you live.

PART II

Getting on with Life

6

Day-to-Day Coping Strategies

Setting the Attitude for Your Household

Do you ever feel that your child's disability is the single factor that determines how things are going to go in your home every day? Have dealing with recurrent respiratory infections, struggling with medication schedules, or fighting over physical therapy sessions taken the joy out of your home?

Believe it or not, you can choose to improve the quality of life you and your family enjoy every (or almost every) day. Throughout this book, and especially this chapter, you will find information about how to access help to make those tough days a little more bearable.

One key is to maintain your sense of humor. Remember, the things you find funny now might be situations that you might have found uncomfortable not long ago.

For instance, a mother and her child, who was partially paralyzed, flew across the country for a family event. Although everyone was tired, they went out to eat with the aunt and cousin at a family-style restaurant. Everyone ordered lunch, including the daughter who was tired from the trip. Just as lunch was served, the little girl looked at her meal, looked at everyone at the table, and fell face forward into her french fries. An embarrassing moment? At the time, yes. Did it become a family story that always got a laugh? Absolutely.

Keep Your Perspective

You need to keep a handle on which problems are yours and which are really your child's. As much as you want to, you cannot protect your child from every emotional hurt that comes with growing up. The best gift you can give your child in these circumstances is the emotional resources to deal with his own problems.

One of the hardest parts of being a parent for Cathy is keeping her feelings in check so she can listen to her son's problems while supporting his needs rather than venting her feelings. Born with a bilateral cleft palate, Roger comes home devastated when kids on the school bus call him names, including "pig nose." While it really hurts Cathy to see him feel so bad, she says that she has found that Roger feels most supported when she simply listens to his problems and acknowledges his pain. She says that when she gets angry at the people who hurt him, he stops coming to her for help because he wants to protect her feelings.

Be Consistent

Also keep in mind that the behavior standards you set for your child should be enforced in public as much as at home. After all, wouldn't you hold your child to the same behavioral standards at home and away if he weren't disabled?

One mother of two disabled children often had to take both of them to the grocery store when she did her regular shopping. The young, school-aged boys saw the grocery store as a wide-open opportunity to race their electric wheelchairs, play hide-and-seek, and generally have a great time. Because the kids got so much pleasure from these times—and they were careful not to plow into other shoppers—their mom tended to let them enjoy themselves. However, there were a few times when they got out of hand. Then, knowing they needed to be reined in, she sometimes told them that if they didn't quit running around and stay with her, she was going to unplug them. Effective? Yes. Did other shoppers drop their jaws in surprise? Yes. But she felt that the need to teach her children to behave and act responsibly was more important than the reaction of strangers.

Dealing with Chronic Sorrow

You have undoubtedly heard (or will hear) about or read about the emotional stages parents can go through in dealing with their child and her disability. Studying these stages can be very helpful. However, when people interpret the stage of "acceptance" as meaning that there is no longer any emotional turmoil, they are setting themselves up for trouble. Most people will have varying degrees of chronic sorrow for the rest of their lives as they raise their children and deal with the disability.

Even when things are going along fairly smoothly, it is normal to be reminded that your life is irrevocably different from that of many other families. It may be the small things that surprise you with their sting. Maybe your son who lost a leg to cancer does not make first string on the football team like his dad did. Maybe you have given up tennis because you can't stand seeing your child sitting on the sidelines in a wheelchair while you chase balls. Maybe you are torn to the core when you praise one child for achieving a physical goal that you realize his sibling will never accomplish. It may even be something remarkably simple like a birthday celebration that becomes bittersweet because you are grateful that your child has lived this long, but also sad that she has not been able to have the experiences you had at that age.

Many people continue to experience a level of chronic sorrow. This does not mean that they are failing to make a healthy emotional adjustment to their child's problems. It does mean that they are normal and that they realize that their child's disability is not something that happened in the past; it is an ongoing part of their lives today.

The good news is that things usually do improve over time. One possible explanation is that you build emotional "callouses" over the hurting parts. These callouses enable you to keep handling the difficult moments because you know that you have done it before and you are strong enough to do it again. You also will find that as your child grows and becomes even more important in your life—to the point that you cannot imagine life without him—the differences become somewhat less important than the joy you get from having him with you.

Remember that even when you think your emotional life is under control, the feelings are always there—waiting to come to the surface. The things that may trigger an emotional response for you may not even be things you have given much conscious thought to. It could be as simple as seeing your child's peers going off to go swimming, but your child cannot go in the pool without an adult to hold her up. Maybe it is having your child reach that magic age when all his friends are getting their driver's licenses, but you realize that your child's disability prevents him from driving safely. Perhaps there is some other dream or expectation for your child that will never be achieved.

Give yourself permission to accept the difficult feelings when they crop up. When you find it particularly difficult to deal with the disappointments, consider talking with other parents whose children have disabilities and who understand the feelings you are struggling with today. It won't change the reality you are living with, but it will help you remember that you are not alone.

How to Develop a Great Support Network

By the time you are past the immediate stress of the diagnostic process, you've probably already started wondering how you are going to handle everything. This is the time to build on the support network you already have in place and design new layers to your network to meet the needs you are just discovering.

Your current support network is probably made up of family and friends along with a smattering of medical professionals. These people will form the backbone of your support network. You will discover there are others who will be eager to help once you let your needs be known.

Reach Outside Your Family

Have you thought of talking with other parents who are dealing with the same problems you have but who may be further along the road?

They can be a great source of emotional support as well as practical information. Sometimes you will be amazed at the information you pick up in even the most casual conversation with other parents.

A Canadian woman whose child uses diapers because of her spina bifida was chatting with another parent and discovered that her family was eligible to receive a subsidy to cover the cost of the diapers. A California mom of a teenager found out from another parent that the State Department of Rehabilitation would help cover a significant amount of the cost of sending her child to a university.

There are many ways to find these families. One note: confidentiality is a very important concept in medical care. Doctors, therapists, and others will not be able to give you the name and phone number of a family unless that family has already given them permission to give out that information. One way to handle that is to ask the medical professional to give your name to the other families and ask them to call you. (If it is likely to incur toll charges, you might even offer to take collect calls as a courtesy.) If the family has given the medical professional permission to give its name out, that person may request that you call the family the first time. (It can be a way of being sure that you really want the contact and are not being pressured into it.)

Some Typical Ways to Find Peer Support

Following are some suggestions for locating peer support.

Ask Your Doctor. Your child's primary care physician or specialists may be able to put you in touch with other families in your geographical area.

Ask Your Hospital Social Worker. This person may be in touch with families being served by many physicians at the facility and may also be in touch with a variety of community groups that could be useful to you.

Call National Organizations. Start with the list in Appendix 2. If you don't have a specific diagnosis yet or don't see an organization with the right name, start with the likely places. For instance, the Muscular Dystrophy Association deals with 40 neuromuscular diseases, not just Duchenne muscular dystrophy. If your doctor has used general terms like "neuromuscular disease," MDA may be able to help you. If you are dealing with a birth defect, the March of Dimes may be the place to start. Whichever organization you call, ask for the patient services department and there should be someone there who can either help you or direct you to a more appropriate organization.

Ask at Your Local School District. The head of your local special education department is likely to know of other families and/or organizations. Some special education schools and classes have parent support groups. Again, remember that school districts also have confidentiality constraints so they may have to take your name and pass it on rather than giving you the information you want directly.

Write to Exceptional Parent *Magazine.* This wonderful magazine is available by subscription and offers families insight into and information on all aspects of raising a child who is disabled. One unique benefit the magazine offers is that parents can write in and ask to have other families dealing with the same diagnosis contact them. These letters are regularly published in the magazine, and in the "Parents Respond" section, parents answer questions raised in previous issues. Other departments include "Fun Stuff," "Fathers' Voices," "Point of View," "Children's Page," and "Corporations Who Care." As of this writing, the subscription rate for 12 issues is $24 in the U.S. and $30 in Canada. You can call for information about *Exceptional Parent* magazine at (800)247-8080.

I Want Help Now!

The very day Opal gave birth and discovered that her son had a complete cleft palate, she knew she needed to talk with other parents who could help her understand what she and her child had ahead of them. Somewhat originally (if not successfully), she first reached for the phone book to see if any organizations were listed. However, her second thought worked better: Opal called the teachers at her child-birth classes. Since they worked with a lot of recent new mothers, they were able to put her in touch with several other families who were also dealing with cleft palate problems.

As you deal with different organizations, you will find that some have parent support groups you will be invited to join. They range from formal, organized groups with officers, programs, and even therapists to informal get-togethers, to groups that focus on raising funds for research. Each type of group has its individual strengths and you are likely to meet helpful people at any one of them.

The parents you meet through support groups will be an important addition to your personal network. On some days, it can really help to talk to someone who has already lived through the stages you and your child are going through. People you meet there can also be a tremendous resource in a pinch. Who else would you call when your van breaks down and your child and his wheelchair need a lift home?

Be Cautious About Who You Trust

Over time, your network will grow to include people who touch every facet of your life. But there are some situations you need to be careful about.

First, no one has a right to tell you what to do just because they have helped or offered to help you. There are, unfortunately, some people in the world who are best called "users." They want to use you to make themselves feel virtuous and/or powerful.

If you find that someone is making demands on you (i.e., "You should do what I tell you because I've been so good to you."), you should consider seriously whether you want to continue that relationship. If you are confused about whether the relationship is becoming unhealthy, talk it over with a friend or professional whose opinion you respect.

Second, be cautious about people who try to convince you that if you just use their product, pray the way they pray, or seek out the miraculous cure they heard about everything will be fine again. These are situations where your support network can really pay off.

If the product sounds good, talk to your child's medical professionals about it. They can tell you (or research and then tell you) how any given product or treatment is likely to affect your child—and whether it is dangerous.

Prayer is a powerful tool for help and support, but if there were one specific way to pray that cured everything, don't you think everyone would already be using it? Talk it over with your pastor, priest, rabbi, or other spiritual counselor. If you don't have one in your personal network, most hospitals have clergy who would be glad to meet with you.

Some of the suggestions people offer can fall into the category of alternative medicine. Perhaps you are asked to consider accupressure therapy, acupuncture therapy, or other therapies that fall outside traditional Western medical treatments. Some of these therapies have been shown to be useful, but not in all situations. Talk with your medical team to be sure you understand the pros and cons of any alternative treatments before you begin them. For instance, megavitamins are sometimes said to have certain curative powers, but too much of some vitamins can cause serious new problems and even lead to death.

The kinds of help covered in this section are only the start of what you can expect from your support network. You will be amazed at how helpful people can be if you just tell them what you need.

If you feel restrained by that old saying, "It is more blessed to give than receive," and you believe that by receiving help from others that you are somehow less than you want to appear, stop it right now.

Think back to a time when you felt good because you had helped someone you cared about with something important. Well, your half of the giving in the situation you are coping with now is that you are giving someone else the gift of an opportunity to share with you in the same way you have helped others before.

One last thought on this. Don't get greedy. Ask for what you need, but don't abuse the people who want to help—you may need them again later.

Getting Validation of Your Parenting Experience

Unless you and your child live alone in a cave, you will come in contact with other families with children your child's age. Frequently, the conversation at these times tends to turn to comparisons of the achievements of everyone's kids. "My Arthur is walking at 10 months!" "My Susie's dance teacher says she has real talent."

While these parents are understandably proud of their child's progress, if and when they remember that you are standing there with the group, you are likely to hear, "Well, we know it's different for you," (especially if your child's physical disability keeps him from achieving the same milestones). Somehow you suspect (or have found through experience) that adding that your son's physical therapy for Duchenne has kept him out of a wheelchair longer than expected or that your daughter has learned to give herself insulin shots can be a real conversation killer. When this time comes, there are two things for you to remember:

1. They don't mean to make you feel left out. Conversations about the milestones children achieve is a way of getting validation of their parenting experience.

2. Your close friends really will want to hear about every milestone your child achieves and every setback you have to deal with just as you really want to hear about how their children are doing.

Like any other parent, you also want to feel that your parenting efforts are recognized by your peers. This is when your support network is especially valuable. If you've had a depressing day at the pediatrician's office where your two-year-old was the only one in the waiting room not walking or something else has happened that has led to your feeling down, get in touch with someone in your network. Maybe it will be a friend or relative who really listens. Maybe you should bring it up when you are talking to your pediatrician. Perhaps the best person to reassure you about how you are doing is another parent who is dealing with the same disability. Don't expect others to magically know that you are having a tough day and reach out to you.

When you take the first step to let them know what you need, you will be in a much better position to get the support that will help you get through the day.

Try to See the Humor in the Situation

Sometimes people ask the most outrageous questions or make the most ridiculous statements and you find yourself wavering between laughing out loud and getting really angry. The best recourse is usually to try to see the humor, whether it was intended or not. As my husband often says about these situations, "Violence is only a momentary pleasure and is likely to get you arrested." Some parents report having people ask them, "What did you do to your child?" Others have been told how nice it was for them to take those poor dears for an outing when the family, which included two children with disabilities simply went to the grocery store. Several parents have suggested that there were times that they wanted to deck people for the things they have said, but, instead, added the comments to their personal list of "stupid human sayings."

Sharing the insensitive comments with others who understand what you are going through or making them into family jokes will help you put them in perspective. There may be times when you can educate someone who has said something insensitive (OK, something stupid) by teaching them about your child's disability. However, remember that it is not your job to educate the whole world. At times, it is better just to ignore some people and focus your energy on the people and events that are important to your family.

You can also look inside yourself. When you know that you are doing your best, give yourself the credit you deserve. Your parenting experience is valid and valuable. In time, when you look back on these days, you may find they opened doors to understanding your own strengths and talents in a way you can use to expand your future and your child's.

But for today, if you are feeling sad and left out when it comes to being recognized for your parenting skills, take heart. The fact that you have been—and continue to be—a hard-working, loving person who struggles to meet all your child's varied and sometimes overwhelming needs makes you one of life's truly great parents. And nothing can take that away from you.

Balancing Your Responsibilities

Wouldn't life be great if your only concern was taking care of your disabled child? However, in real life, you are probably also dealing with other children, a spouse, your parents/in-laws, your job, friends, and who knows what else. In fact, a recent study published in a medically oriented journal found that only 26 percent of the families whose children were chronically ill had a traditional nuclear family with the father as breadwinner and the mother as a full-time home-maker.

Believe it or not, you still have choices (even though some of them may be tongue-in-cheek). You can try to please everyone else (doomed to failure—the more you do, the more they expect). You can simply give up, but you are not likely to get any of the results you really hope for that way.

More than likely, you will try to strike a balance between what you feel others expect of you, what you expect of yourself, and what is realistically possible. As you are balancing your responsibilities, you will have to integrate the goals you have defined for your child along with the goals you have for yourself, other family members, and the family as a whole.

Making Time for Things That Really Matter

Start by writing a list of everything you think you should be doing, including the things you are actually accomplishing right now. Make the list detailed. Start with the morning activities like fixing breakfast, bathing and dressing your child(ren), and packing lunches. Make your list go through the whole day. Now add the things you wish you could find time for and the things others (maybe medical professionals) have told you that you should be doing every day. Put a checkmark next to the activities that are most important for the health and happiness of your family. What's left?

You may discover that you are spending hours every day on

activities that do not have a high priority for you, leaving you less time for the things that are actually more important. Maybe you find that you are spending two hours a day keeping the house spotless, but don't have time to read to your kids before bedtime. Unless someone in your house has a real physical allergy to dust, everyone is likely to be happier if you forego the cleaning sometimes and have an evening story hour.

In addition, review regular tasks to see if some of them can be delegated or ignored without serious consequences. If family members take their clean underwear and socks and stuff them in the drawer without folding them, the world as we know it will not end, but you have just saved some time every week folding laundry. Children can do all sorts of small jobs to help out, anything from setting the table to sweeping the front sidewalk. And unless you overwhelm them with work, having responsibilities they are expected to fulfill teaches them a lot about being part of a family team.

Don't Forget Your Partner

If you are married or have a partner, there is no reason why that person cannot help you to strike a balance in your responsibilities and give you time for activities that are valuable to you just as your partner wants to have time for activities that are valuable to him.

You might start with a nonthreatening discussion about what you are hoping will happen. Do you want his help so you will have some time and energy to spend with him once the kids are in bed at night? Tell him and work together to find a balance that allows both of you some leisure time. Maybe one of you does the dishes and the other bathes the children. If you both love to spend time playing with the kids in the tub and hate doing dishes, maybe you could switch off every other night. On the other hand, if you are home with the kids all day, a few quiet moments doing dishes while he handles the baths could be a welcome relief.

If You Are a Single Parent

You may not have others in your home who can take some of the responsibilities over for you. You can, however, make adjustments in your life that will allow you to accomplish the activities that are most important to you. You may have to let the housework slide or consider creative ways to save time (like cooking double batches of dinner and freezing half so you only have to reheat a meal another day). Use the time you save to enjoy some of the activities on your list that you would not have been able to get to otherwise.

The Importance of Respite

It may sound contradictory, but one of the best things you can do for your child is get away from him once in a while. Whether the break is a few hours or a few days at a time, it is very important that you and your child get a breather from each other from time to time because:

> *Taking a break is simply good mental health.* Taking a breather from an intense situation can help you get a new perspective as well as allowing you to return to the fray refreshed from the change of pace. In addition, it is good for your child's mental health; she should have a break from you too. Little children may not feel that way, but older children often will, even if they don't tell you.

> *Taking a break is good for your physical health.* When you feel better emotionally, your body responds to that. If you never have a break from the challenges of caring for your child, you are more likely to have stress-related physical problems such as headaches, stomach aches, and hypertension.

The Respite Care Option

It is very normal to feel that no one else can do what you do for your child. That may be true, but when you find a caregiver who is competent and teach her what she needs to know to give your child good care, your child will be as safe as if you were there. Other caregivers also bring their own personality and experiences that will provide an interesting change for your child.

There may be respite services (which staff childcare so you can get away for a while) available to you through several sources.

Depending on your personal situation, the most desirable might be in-home respite through an agency with the bills being paid by a government agency. In recent years, more than 30 states have passed legislation for in-house family support services which can include respite care. To find out about any programs available to you, check with your state, using the phone number in Appendix 3.

On a less formal level, don't overlook community resources. There may be programs through social service agencies, church "Mom's day out" programs, or informal neighborhood childcare exchanges. You may not be able to schedule these at your convenience, but they can offer a regular break you can look forward to.

Whether you have formal respite services using professional nurses or caregivers through an agency, hire someone yourself, or have friends or family take care of your child so you can get away from time to time, you need to be sure you have made it as safe and enjoyable for your child as possible. You might want to hang around for a while during the first time a new caregiver works with your child to be sure he understands your child's individual needs and is competent. Just keep it brief. The whole idea of respite is to give you a break from your duties, not to give you someone else to supervise.

Choose Caregivers Carefully

If your child's medical condition is such that medical emergencies and/or life-threatening situations are likely to occur, think carefully about who you will chose before you arrange for someone besides yourself to do childcare.

Having older siblings or neighborhood teens act as caregivers will work for many, but not all, families. If there is a possibility that that young person could be put in a position of dealing with emergencies or possible (even natural) death, please see if there are other options you can pursue. In the worst case, the young person could go through life wondering if he somehow caused the emergency and/or death. That is a terrible burden to risk putting on any young person. In these cases, it is better to have an adult as caregiver because an adult is likely to be better able to handle the emotional fallout if the worst happens.

Another respite option to consider is enrolling your child in a good preschool once she is old enough. Such a program will offer you a brief break on a regular schedule (at least enough time to get to the grocery store or get a haircut).

There are two directions you can explore. The first is a regular daycare facility or preschool in your community. The other is a special preschool program through your school district for children who are physically disabled (see chapter 8).

Not many years ago, preschools and daycare centers frequently refused to care for children who had physical disabilities. However, with the passing of the Americans with Disabilities Act, this kind of discrimination is now illegal.

In the event that the daycare provider or center is not equipped to care adequately for your child, you will need to be resourceful to help that provider become equipped or knowledgeable about ways to care for your child. You should do this not because it is your legal responsibility, but because it is your parental responsibility.

You might start by bringing literature about your child's general diagnosis and plan to spend time with the staff explaining your child's individual needs. You might also consider what equipment you might already have that can be loaned to the school during your child's enrollment to make the adjustment easier for everyone.

If you choose a school district program but you do not feel that your child is physically or emotionally ready or strong enough to go every day, you can have your doctor write orders stating that your child will go on whatever schedule the two of you agree on (possibly adding that the number of days per week at school can be altered as you see fit).

Hiring a Respite Worker

You also have the option of hiring someone from an agency to meet your respite needs. This can be very expensive if you do it on your own. However, there are different levels of care requiring different licenses so you will want to talk to the person at the agency who handles new clients to determine the level of care your child will need and what the costs will be. This person may also be able to tell you about government-funded programs (if any) you may be able to access to help pay the bills.

If you decide to hire people on your own, there are several sources you may want to consider. The most obvious would be referrals from friends who hire childcare workers in their home. Be somewhat leery of placing ads since you will have to check references very carefully to be sure they are who they say they are and that they are competent.

Consider contacting employment offices at local nursing schools. Students are often eager to find work in the professional areas they are pursuing. You will get a motivated worker who comes with some basic understanding of medical problems. In addition, consider looking for schools that teach people to become physical therapists or occupational therapists, and even universities that have pre-med programs.

Another option is to contact the local office of the nursing organizations (get a phone number from your hospital social worker). These organizations may have an employment service for active nurses who want more work or they may be able to refer you to retired nurses who are interested in keeping their hand in.

One thing to consider if you are employing nurses or other medical professionals either through an agency or privately is how they dress at your house. Often, these professionals are told to wear white uniforms and name tags when they work in someone's home. That certainly helps them maintain their professional image, but it may have a negative effect on children who are being served by these professionals.

Before the worker comes to your home for the first time, ask her to wear comfortable, casual clothing. You know she is a professional, and she knows she is a professional, but there is no need to advertise the fact. When your child has friends in, or they come to the door when the worker is there, a uniformed caregiver sets your child apart from other children who have childcare workers in their homes.

If you are hiring someone through an agency, it is fine if he wears a name tag until he crosses your threshold. Once he is in your home, he should take off the name tag, partially to appear more like other childcare workers, and partially so he does not scratch your child with it when he picks her up.

A caveat. If you work outside your home, that job can serve some of the same purposes as respite, but don't think it fills all the same needs for you. Working can be wonderful and necessary: wonderful if you enjoy your work and it gives you a mental break from everything going on at home; necessary if you need the income and/or health insurance your job offers to be able to take care of your child the way you want to.

If you are working outside your home, you still will need to plan for times to give you a respite from your responsibilities. Try to make plans for a regular break, perhaps a Friday night out, that you schedule every week whether it is alone, with a spouse, or with friends (or some combination of those). Time to pursue activities just for yourself will help recharge your personal batteries so you will continue to have energy to take care of your family's needs.

Preparation for the Caregiver

Like any parents, you will need to do standard things like leaving the caregiver some emergency phone numbers, food your child likes to eat (and something for the caregiver if it is more than an hour or two), plenty of diapers (if necessary) or other personal care items.

The Caregiver's Notebook

Because of your unique situation, other things are not quite so standard. You might want to keep a loose-leaf notebook to hold all the information a caregiver will want to know (but might be afraid to ask). This is especially important if your child is very young or has problems with speech or communication.

The first page should list all the names and phone numbers of people the caregiver might need in an emergency or urgent situation. These could include your child's primary physician and specialists. Also add nearby relatives, neighbors, or others who are familiar with your child and his needs.

Depending on the extent of your child's disability, you might want to include a page or two outlining his medical history.

Be sure to include a listing of his current medications. Give the description from the container (name of medication, strength, how much to take, and how often). In addition, note any allergies you know he has to foods, medications, and so on. Update this when there are changes.

Have a signed letter authorizing medical treatment in the event of an emergency. You absolutely should have signed forms on file with your child's doctor and the hospital(s) he is most likely to be taken to in an emergency so there will not be any delays in treatment, but this may come in useful, too.

Provide special handling instructions. Does your child require specific positioning, special attention to hearing aids or glasses, or other care techniques that may not be familiar to the caregiver? Are there special ways your child likes to be handled at bath- or bedtime? Is there any special pulmonary care routine that needs to be followed? (If so, be sure you have demonstrated it to the caregiver; these instructions are just for backup.) Consider including a few photos of how things are supposed to look if you think it will help.

Include a page or two outlining fun activities they can do together especially if your child is very young or has problems communicating verbally. Some activities should be for indoors (i.e., toys, games, and books) and others for outside (walks, playgrounds). Include instructions for finding and manipulating any equipment that will be necessary (such as strollers or wheelchairs).

One final thought. There is one more page you need to write. Accidents can happen to anyone. Your child's caregiver should have a letter (leave it sealed, if you want) that tells her what to do if something happens and you do not return. If you have a respite agency, be sure they have a note in their files that the letter exists and where it can be found. Then, if you are injured, ill, or worse, they have your instructions about who should take responsibility for your child. Otherwise, your child may end up in protective custody or in a hospital while the authorities try to decide what needs to be done.

If you use a respite agency, tuck the forms they want to keep at your house and any time sheets in this notebook so everything will be together. Then keep it somewhere easy to reach so it can be used frequently.

The Influence of Your Spiritual Beliefs

You are undoubtedly finding that part of dealing with your child's disability involves reexamining your own spiritual values. Our society often tries to keep spiritual concerns completely separate from day-to-day living. Yet, at the same time, references to spirituality are everywhere.

Many of us find that a personal crisis (especially death or disability) causes us to review and challenge our long-held beliefs. If we see life as preordained, we want to change the script. If we see God as a loving father, we want a big favor from "Dad"—things back the way they were supposed to be. Those of us who see God as vengeful want to find the magic word or act that will appease Him. Even those of us who do not believe in a higher power are still likely to want to find some order in the universe that will make sense of the situation we currently find ourselves living in.

While there are cases of miraculous cures, most of us are not likely to see their child's disability suddenly and miraculously cured, no matter how strong our faith.

However, many of us will look back after some time has passed and feel that we have been blessed with many of what could be called minor miracles: a friend who listens to you rant and rave after a particularly hard day; a respite worker who tackles that big stack of laundry for you even though it was not in her job description; a car mechanic who drops everything to fix your engine so you can get to the hospital to visit your child. Real people? Yes. Real angels? You decide.

It would be nice if the most difficult part of dealing with your spiritual beliefs was deciding whether or not there were angels helping you handle your problems. However, for many of us, the spiritual crisis we face when we discover that our child is disabled is much more serious. We wonder why God is making us go through all of this. Have we somehow done something to anger God and this is our punishment? Worse, have we done something to anger God and He is punishing our child?

Words That Hurt

Adding to the problem are well-meaning people who thoughtlessly say things that are more likely to add to your anguish than comfort you. A favorite(?) phrase parents recall is, "God must have loved you a lot to give you such a special child." One mother who remembered this said she was very tempted to respond that maybe God should have loved her child a little less, but she realized that the speaker did not realize she wasn't making any sense. Was the mom supposed to believe that if God didn't love a child he made it perfectly healthy?

Another is, "It's God's will." Some parents find comfort in that phrase; others will decide that the God they believe in does not go around crippling little children. These days when there are so many medical treatments that can prolong life and alleviate disabling conditions, many families choose to believe that God's will is that humans find ways of treating and curing disabilities, not just living with them.

Then there is the phrase, "There but for the grace of God go I." One parent I know (who considers herself to be religious) admits that she gets very angry at people who say this to her. She wonders, do the speakers think that God loves them more because they are not dealing with disability—and does their God think its a good idea for them to be telling these other parents that they are not in His good graces?

On the other hand, there are people who can bring their religious or spiritual beliefs into a conversation in a way that is comforting when times are tough. Many parents say that phrases like, "I'll pray for you," or "God bless you," can be a real comfort.

Where to Look for Answers

So, what can you do if you are confused about how God and religion fit into your life right now? Here are some time-honored techniques you can try.

Read. Start with your Bible, Torah, Koran, or other sacred writings. Most large bookstores also have a religious section that has current books written in everyday language about all aspects of faith and religion.

Talk. You can start with spiritual professionals (pastors, priests, rabbis, and so on). If you find that you have philosophical differences with the first person you talk to, keep looking. Like doctors, therapists, or other professionals who deal with very personal subjects, you will find you get along better with some spiritual professionals than others. If you do not have a personal spiritual counselor, you can usually find a chaplain at your hospital who can talk with you or refer you to someone you are likely to find helpful. You might also find it helps to identify lay people you know whose spiritual values you admire and talk with them.

Give yourself time. People who are seeking spiritual answers say they are going on a spiritual "journey," a phrase which acknowledges that you will not reach your goal overnight. Recognize that (if you are smart and lucky) you will continue to see your views mature throughout your lifetime. Just as there are many varieties of flowers or butterflies, there are many spiritual paths that bring people to a sense of peace about their life. Take the time to explore the paths that feel right to you.

The Children Are Watching

Just as you are embarking on your own spiritual journey, you are leading your children through the first steps of their own journey. It is important to recognize your own spiritual beliefs and pass them on to your children. Children are curious and usually believe what you tell them. If you say they have a guardian angel on their shoulder, they may give it a name. If you tell them heroic stories from your religious heritage, they will absorb the values those stories teach.

Please do not feel that your children do not need to know about your spiritual beliefs. Kids have questions, especially children who are dealing with disabilities of their own and who have siblings or friends who are disabled.

The unfortunate fact is that children who have disabilities are more likely to die or have disabled friends who die than average children. When that subject comes up, your child will want to know what you think happens "after." If you know this subject is likely to come up soon, you may want to talk with your spiritual counselor about ways to share your beliefs with your child.

One last thought. There are some people who, for whatever reason, will try to use your situation to improve their own spiritual self-image. They may want to tell you how to pray, what church or activities to participate in, or in some other way try to control your life. They may want to pray over your children when they see you in shopping centers or convert you to their religion "for your own good."

By and large, these people are usually more interested in *appearing* to be good, religious people and making brownie points with their God than in really helping you. It is often best to thank them kindly for their interest, firmly advise them that you prefer they pray for your child at their home, not in the mall, and focus your attention on your own spiritual beliefs. You do not owe them anything, and if their beliefs are very different from your own, it can be very confusing to your child if you humor these people.

When all is said and done, remember that spiritual values and faith are not something your dust off once a week or a couple of times a year. What you really believe is going to be evident by the way you live your life every day. As tough as times are right now, you are likely to find that the spiritual questions you ask and the journey you undertake will lead you to personal growth and a deeper understanding of your spiritual self.

7

Living Life to the Fullest

As the lines from Ecclesiastes so eloquently say, "To everything there is a season, and a time for every purpose under heaven. . . . A time to weep, and a time to laugh; a time to mourn, and a time to dance." Especially in the early months and years of handling your child's disability, you may find the scales of life weighed down by the weeping and mourning with precious little left for the laughing and dancing.

Few sane people would choose to ignore the difficulties in their lives and focus only on the laughing and dancing. But you do need to strike some sort of balance between the sorrow and the joy so that you and your child can take pleasure in the opportunities that are there for you.

This chapter contains some ideas for enjoying your life today, making the social world a better place for your child, and benefiting from some possibilities you may not have thought of. You may be able to use some of these ideas just as they are, or they may spark ideas that are more suitable for your family's needs. As Tevye said in *Fiddler on the Roof,* "L' Chaim"—To Life!

The Gift of Sensory Stimulation

You might be surprised to learn that lack of sensory experiences can affect how your child fares on standardized evaluations. For instance, when a three-year-old girl in Illinois was being evaluated, she could not identify what a drum was for and the tester marked that against her cognitive score. Up to that point, her parents had considered it a plus that she was not banging on a drum, but by that evening, they made sure she had a drum of her own so she would understand what a drum really did in her next evaluation.

As you become more aware of the educational, social, and sensory value of giving your child opportunities to experience new sensations, you will begin to discover opportunities all around you—and both of you will have a lot of fun exploring them.

For example, if you are reading your child a story that mentions characters lying in the grass watching the birds fly by, you undoubtedly have a memory of how grass feels when you sit or lie on it. Has your son experienced the soft way grass can tickle his skin? If he uses a wheelchair, he may never have touched grass. You may need to lift him out of his chair in your yard or local park to give him that sensation. But, if putting him in the grass is not possible, maybe you can take off his shoes and socks and let his feet dangle in a grassy area.

Touch

Touching is one of the most basic human needs. Studies have repeatedly shown that young children who do not receive the stimulation of human touch fail to thrive and sometimes even die.

With a child with a physical disability, you can provide this sensory stimulation in many ways. Obviously, when you are feeding, bathing, dressing, and handling other needs for your child, you are making physical contact. Sometimes these demands can be so overwhelming that anything more seems to present an impossible burden. Yet, your child needs to experience many of the same sensations that others enjoy. These sensations serve both to stimulate and socialize her to the collective understandings people normally expect of each other.

The Sense of Motion

You only have to watch children at a playground to know how much they love to be in motion. When a child has a physical disability, that motion is much more precious simply because it is so rare. You can give your child that sensation of motion in many ways.

One mother whose quadriplegic daughter was often in the hospital connected to IVs found a special way to handle the painful and frightening time when a floor nurse removed the old IV because the site had "blown" and the IV nurse was sent up to start a new one. The mom distracted her daughter from the upcoming pain by focusing on her love of motion. For those few moments, she picked up her daughter and the two of them waltzed or polkaed around the room or the nurses' station. Singing quietly to themselves, they swirled and dipped until they were both breathless. Admittedly, staff people were sometimes puzzled by the commotion, but it was powerful medicine for her daughter.

You do not have to wait for a hospitalization to dance with your child. If he is small, carry him. Dance to whatever makes you both smile. Rhythmic dances like waltzes and polkas give a physical understanding to following patterns. Dancing to rock music may not follow a pattern as much as it feels the beat. Young children also will enjoy activity songs like, "I'm a Little Teapot." You can assist them in positioning and movement as they dance to the song.

If your child is too large to carry, have him sit on your lap and the two of you can sway to the music. If he uses crutches or a wheelchair, spend time with him creating ways he can use them to help him respond to the music. Then dance with him! You both will enjoy the experience.

When time allows, consider going to a local playground and sharing that sensory experience with your child. Simple activities might include playing in the sandbox and feeling the gritty texture and the sun-baked warmth. You can lift your small child part way up a sliding board and gently guide him as he slides down. Swings give a wonderful feeling of freedom. A small child or one who cannot grasp the chains can be held on your lap while the two of you gently swing.

Because of the potential for injury, you will need to be especially careful on a playground. Seesaws and merry-go-rounds can be dangerous if your child is not strong enough to hang on to them. Be sure to ride with him or stand next to him and spot him until you are sure of his ability. If you have a physical therapist, she can be helpful in evaluating your child's ability to handle playground equipment.

The Ultimate Playgrounds: Amusement Parks

Certainly the ultimate playground is an amusement park because it combines all types of sensory stimulation. Whatever your child's level of physical ability, there will be new sights, sounds, smells, and sensations to thrill her. Many parks have active attractions like rides and more passive attractions like stage shows. Plan to keep a balance so neither you nor your child become overly exhausted.

If you have any question about whether a particular ride is safe and appropriate, ride it alone once to determine if it is safe for your child. For instance, a ride that exerts strong "G" forces as it swings in circles may cause you to slide on the seat. Ascertain if you can hold your child safely without her slipping out or getting a body slam from you as you slide.

For weak children, the safest rides are normally the ones that do not need safety restraints, such as merry-go-rounds, and any ride where you are completely enclosed in a seating container that moves gently. If you are considering taking your child on a thrill ride such as a roller coaster, talk with your doctor or physical therapist first and, if you must make a decision, err on the side of caution.

Avoiding Lines. Many parks have special entrances to rides and attractions for families with a child who is disabled. Often you can bypass the long lines and be accommodated almost immediately. However, some parks now have a policy that only one person may accompany the child. Others have to go through the line and you will all be accommodated when they get to the front of the line. In theory it makes sense, but it can be pretty boring for the person who spends most of the day alone standing in line. Check with the park about its regulations before you go.

Meeting Restroom Needs. In all likelihood, the park will have some extra-large restroom stalls marked for people who have disabilities. However, if your particular equipment and maneuvering needs do not permit you to use these stalls discretely, help is usually available. Look for a nursing or first-aid station. It should have a bathroom and/or private area with beds and bedpans where you can help your child with her toileting needs. The staff may be willing to lend a hand if you need help.

There are sensory opportunities around you every day. Your child will love the feeling of a soft kitten on her lap, puppy licks on her face, or even a wiggling worm in her hand. Make sure you help her experience as much of life as you can.

Wishes That Work

As mentioned in chapter 6, you have probably already noticed that there are times when you need the help of other people. There also will be times when someone else is able to offer something wonderful for your child that you cannot manage yourself. The organizations that grant the wishes of children who have serious, chronic, or life-threatening medical conditions have done marvelous things for many families. You may think a child has to be on death's door to receive the benefits of these programs, but that is not necessarily true.

Make-A-Wish Foundation®

The Make-A-Wish Foundation is the best known of these organizations. Any child under 18 years old who has been determined by a physician to have a terminal illness or life-threatening medical condition that creates the probability that the child will not survive beyond his or her 18th year is eligible.

Parents, legal guardians, medical professionals working with the child, or even the child can make the initial contact. Call the national office at (800)722-9474 for referral to a local chapter that will coordinate qualifying wishes.

During the initial local telephone conversation, a Make-A-Wish Foundation representative will explain both the purpose of the organization and the medical qualifications to become a wish recipient. Then, if it appears that a child will qualify, a wish team of volunteers will be assigned to the child. The team visits the child and the family to determine what the child's dearest wish is. The child's physician is contacted to be sure the wish can be fulfilled. The volunteers submit the wish to the chapter board of directors and then the wish team gets busy making it all come true.

Make-A-Wish works hard to make each child's dream a reality. Most of the wishes are fairly predictable. Roughly half of the children request a trip to Disney World or Disneyland. The majority of wishes tend to fit into one of four categories: places they want to go, things they want to be, people they want to meet, or things they want to have.

When possible, the immediate family is included. All expenses are covered, including travel and spending money. That way the whole family can make joyful memories without worrying about the expenses of making the wish come true.

While each child's story is unique, Gail's experience is one example of how a child's wish has been granted. Gail has a disability that has left her nearly totally paralyzed. When she was 11 years old, life was tough. Her sister (who had the same diagnosis) had recently died, leaving the whole family devastated. There was also some worry that her father's job might not last much longer, the way the economy was going. To say the least, it was a difficult time.

When a friend told Gail's mother about Make-A-Wish, she called the organization. The representative took the background information and arranged a time to meet with the family.

During their visit, one volunteer talked with the parents and another visited with Gail in a different room. Their reasoning was that it was important to be sure that the wish they filled was actually Gail's and not something Gail thought her family wanted.

Well, Gail wanted a hot tub/spa for the back yard (which the parents knew about, but could not afford) and she wanted it in a redwood gazebo (which the parents did not know!). Gail had had a chance to use other people's spas before and knew how good it felt (especially for her tight muscles) to sit way down in the warm water and let the jets massage her back and legs.

The Make-A-Wish Foundation people set the wheels in motion and before long there was a shiny new spa (with a redwood gazebo) in the back yard. It has not only proven to be a wonderful way to relax and exercise tight muscles, it has also been a fun place for Gail to get together with her friends.

Your child may want something else. The important thing is that a dream your child dearly wants (and that you may not be able to provide) is fulfilled. With the Make-A-Wish Foundation, only one wish per child is granted.

This organization zealously guards privacy, so you can be sure that unless you choose to let it be known, no one will ever know how you made your child's wish come true.

Other Wish Organizations

There are other wonderful, successful, and generous wish-granting organizations you might contact. Your hospital social worker or disability-related organization should be able to refer you to groups in your area. When you have contacted a wish-granting organization and they have agreed to help your child, you will have the joy of seeing your child's dearest wish come true—and you will have the help of dedicated volunteers to make that wish possible.

A caution: As sad as it is, a few organizations collect a lot of money, but spend virtually none on granting the wishes of disabled and/or dying children. Just because you see a canister saying the organization is raising monies to grant children's wishes, it does not mean that this is an organization you should contact. Before you get your child's and your hopes up about an organization that you are not familiar with, contact your local Better Business Bureau, the Council of Better Business Bureaus at (703)276-0100, or the National Charities Information Bureau at (212)929-6300 to be sure they do what they promise.

Fostering Your Child's Self-Acceptance

One of the hardest and most important jobs you face is helping your child build self-esteem. When people (especially children) have good self-esteem, they are better prepared to face the large and small challenges of life. Wouldn't it be great if you could just give your child all the self-esteem he needs? Well, you can't *give* it to him, but you can certainly help him acquire it for himself.

While you can contribute to how your child feels about himself, he will have to develop that strong core of self-confidence from his own resources and the way he perceives his place in the world.

Building Self-Esteem

The keys to building self-esteem are knowing that one is loved and feeling that one is capable of doing things.

You can make an important contribution to helping your child realize that he is loved. Telling kids you love them is certainly an important factor. It is surprising how often people assume that the ones they love know it. Unfortunately, this is not always true.

In addition to telling your child that you love him, there are less obvious ways you can help him realize he is loved by you. Complement your child on his best physical and personality features. Does your child have sparkly, laughing eyes, a smile that melts your heart, a contagious giggle, a way with other children or small animals, soft skin, or great freckles? Tell him. When you focus on the things that are right more than the things that are wrong, your child absorbs that positive message.

However, when your child has a physical disability, there will be many situations where he is not capable of doing the same things as his peers and that can have a negative impact on his self-esteem unless you work to counter that feeling.

The key to building your child's self-esteem is to focus on the things that *are* possible. Look for situations that are parallel to activities that peers are participating in such as sports leagues tailored to children who have physical disabilities or Special Olympics. A child who is musical may not be capable of learning to play an instrument, but may be able to join a church choir or school chorus. Skill at computer or video games tends to transcend the barriers that are often caused by physical disabilities.

On occasion, you may be able to turn aspects of your child's disability that would ordinarily be seen by peers as negatives into positives. One child with Tourettes Syndrome who had problems with twitching and head shaking loved to play baseball. She was also a pretty good catcher who tended to confound players on the other team because they could never tell whether she was giving signs to the pitcher or simply displaying a symptom of her condition.

Other self-esteem building activities include:

- Excelling at school work.

- Volunteer work through disability organizations (especially efforts that result in pictures in the newspaper or appearances on television where others will see them and complement your child).

- Participating in activities such as Scouts where there are special recognitions like badges to acknowledge new skills.

Pay attention to your child's personal interests. If he enjoys art, display his creations around the house so he will see that you are proud of his work. If he likes to collect stamps, admire the way he organizes his collection. If he takes good care of the family pet, be sure to let him know that you notice.

Also, unless you really overdo it, it is likely to be a real self-esteem builder if your child hears you telling friends or family about his accomplishments and how proud you are of him.

Helping Your Child to Control the Environment

The ability to control and manipulate the environment definitely helps a child develop self-esteem and self-confidence. Look at the world from your child's perspective, and you will see many opportunities you can make available to her to help her feel in control of the environment. For some children, it might be getting an electric wheelchair which allows them to get around independently. For others, it might be allowing them to make minor decisions in medical settings that give them a feeling of some measure of control over an overwhelming situation.

Every child has the right to feel good about herself and it is your responsibility as a parent to do everything possible to help her attain this goal. If you should find that your child's self-esteem is not what it should be to the extent that it is affecting her ability to enjoy life and succeed at school or other activities, you may need to look to other parents or experienced professionals for guidance. No matter how loving and caring a parent you are, your child will eventually realize that you probably did not grow up with the same set of disabilities or problems, and because of that, she may have a difficult time accepting your advice.

When that happens, your child may be able to accept guidance from someone who is not personally involved in the situation even though he or she is saying exactly the same thing you have been saying for ages. Work with your child's teacher, Scout leader, coach, or other adult whom your child trusts. You might even search for a therapist or counselor who has a similar disability to make it easier for your child to accept that person as understanding her own situation.

Don't wait too long to ask for help or the problem might become ingrained and harder to correct. By nipping the situation in the bud, you can help to rebuild confidence and self-esteem so your child can successfully get on with the business of growing up.

Empowering Your Child to Take Control

"Your child has become very manipulative," was the firm message delivered by an obviously disapproving preschool teacher. The mother sat quietly for a moment. If the teacher could have seen inside the mom's heart, she would have seen a quarterback spiking the ball after a touchdown along with major cheering.

Why the different ways of seeing the situation? The teacher's goal was to create a homogeneous society in the classroom. The mother's goal was to give her daughter the skills necessary to get others to perform the tasks that would enable the child to pursue her dreams in life. It was not her goal to create a manipulative child, but rather to raise a child who could manipulate her environment. She also recognized that, over time, her child would be "put in her place" by peers whenever she got too demanding or unreasonable. This mother was adamant about not raising her daughter to be a compliant cog in the system. She wanted her to have the strength and skills to follow her dreams. You can do the same thing for your child.

Explaining the Disability to Your Child's Friends

Whether your child is born with her disability or it occurs later, her peers will ask questions. You may be surprised at how early your child is ready to handle those situations if you have worked with her. But her ability to handle the questions will depend largely on how you have prepared her.

Start Early

Long before your child is able to explain anything about her disability, she will have heard you talk about it. If you talk about it as a matter of fact and focus more on what your child can do than what she cannot do, she will too. For instance, young children may be satisfied with an answer such as, "Your muscles have a sickness and that's why they don't work right."

As your child goes through elementary school, junior high, and high school, she will usually be the one who is asked questions by her peers. The two things you can do to prepare her are to give her honest information and teach her that she does not owe anyone an answer. You might even try role playing to help her determine what she is comfortable with and how to handle questions she does not want to answer.

For example, a child with a tracheostomy who is comfortable with it might describe it as being like the holes some people have in their ears for earrings, but it is in her neck and it makes it easier for her to breathe. A child with cerebral palsy might say that she was hurt when she was being born and so it is hard to make her arms and legs work right. It is usually best to keep the answer short and simple.

One child who had hemophilia gave a presentation at school about his medical condition and even showed how he gives himself shots when necessary. (Only one student was "grossed-out" and had to leave the room.)

On the other hand, there may be times or situations where your child does not want to talk about her disability at all. Make sure you have worked out a way to handle it. Perhaps she could simply say she does not want to talk about it now or tell the other child to ask you, the teacher, or the school nurse. (If your child refers others to the school nurse or her teacher, be sure you have already talked to them and that they are knowledgeable about the disability.)

At times, other children may react badly to your child because of her disability. If this is in a school setting, you may want to start with a parent-teacher conference to discuss the problem. If that doesn't settle the situation, you should meet with your school district's counselor or psychologist to work out a plan of action. One action could be a disability awareness day or an on-going program to make other students more aware of disabilities in general and your child's disability in particular.

Get Parents Involved

If the problem is among playmates, you may need to talk with their parents. If you are upset, calm down before you talk to anyone and be sure to keep the problem in perspective. If you do this, other parents will want to work with you most of the time.

In rare instances, you might feel that the activities of other children are endangering your child. If so, you must talk to their parents, and, if the behavior continues, tell your child not to play with those children any more. If another child threatens your son or daughter, you may want to talk with a juvenile officer from your local police about the best way to handle the situation.

However, resist the urge to step in and fix every disagreement your child has with others. Developing social skills is one of the major tasks of growing up and no one gets through childhood without some hurt feelings.

Seeing Past the Hardware

The equipment that often comes with disability can be off-putting to adults, but is often a source of fascination for children.

When Katie was mainstreamed for the first grade, she was nervous about how people would react to her electric wheelchair. That first afternoon, she came home all smiles. All the boys in class were enthralled by her chair and many wanted her to drive around the playground while they rode on the back. Her chair turned out to be a terrific ice breaker and helped her start making friends right away.

Service dogs that help children who are blind or have other disabilities also help break the ice. They provide a focus for starting conversations with new people.

Fortunately for many children, their peers often take on the job of educating new kids in school or the neighborhood. So, if you move or your child is assigned to a new school, you may need to start from scratch. Talk with the teacher at the new school and work together to create any disability-awareness activities that may be needed. And be sure to take time to discuss the changes with your child and reinforce her confidence in her ability to handle herself in new situations.

Finally, remember that beyond the obvious signs of her disability, how much or how little other information about that disability your child decides to share with friends is ultimately up to her. By allowing that, you are helping her build the ability to handle her world, understand her right to privacy, and gain self-respect.

Developing Social Skills

Children who have school, physical therapy, occupational therapy, and a host of medical/educational activities still need the very special kind of learning that comes from interacting with their peers. This is where they absorb the social skills that will help them succeed in life.

Letting your child participate in community activities (everything from impromptu neighborhood games to more formalized activities like Scouting, 4-H, or sports leagues) is a surprisingly difficult step for some parents. After all, it's not all good times, winning badges, and making new friends. Sometimes it is learning how it feels to fail, what it's like to be the one not invited to the party, and what it's like to be the last one chosen for the team. When your child is already coping with a disability, the potential for adding any other difficulties can be something you would really rather avoid.

As adults, it is easy for us to forget how really tough it is to be a kid—even without the challenge of a physical disability. Unfortunately, that disability does not exempt your child from having to go through the same social learning process as everyone else. The good news is that you can help smooth the process if you start early.

When your child is preschool age, look into entering him in play groups that are organized in your neighborhood or through a mothers' group in your area. Your community may have special play groups for at-risk children through social service departments. Enroll her in Sunday School or other religious groups where she will get to interact with other children on a weekly basis. Encourage older siblings or neighborhood children to spend time playing with him (and don't hover!).

As your child grows, so do the opportunities. Ask if he is interested in Scouting, 4-H, YMCA, Boys Clubs, music lessons, sports leagues (if your child's disability is orthopedic, many communities now have special sports leagues for kids living with orthopedic disabilities), or activities offered through your community recreation department. Often your child will be especially interested in activities he hears classmates talk about.

Call the adults in charge of the organizations your child is interested in and ask them about the kinds of activities they normally do. Ask about any accommodations your child will need such as help with toileting on camp-outs or a designated base runner on the baseball team. If the activity sounds like something that your child can succeed at, encourage him to give it a try.

Another resource for finding out about a wide range of sporting opportunities is to contact National Handicapped Sports (NHS). This nationwide network of 85 community-based chapters and affiliates offers exciting activities for youth and adults such as snow skiing, water skiing, sailing, white water rafting, canoeing, kayaking, bicycling, golf, horseback riding, and aerobic fitness classes. You can call NHS at (301)217-0960 or write them at 451 Hungerford Drive, Suite 100, Rockville, MD 20850.

You may want to be involved in the organization your child participates in, but remember to make the experience as normal as possible. One California mother (who had always looked forward to being a Girl Scout leader) balanced the situation out by being the troop leader during the school year, but during summer camp, she worked in the supply hut so her medically fragile daughter would have the experience of having a different leader while she was still nearby in case she was needed.

Most activities that kids get involved in are actually parent-intensive. Parents become leaders, coaches, or scorekeepers. They get out craft materials or serve refreshments. They organize car pools. Choose the activities that will allow you to achieve the balance you want between giving your child experience at being independent and being nearby yourself in case you are needed.

It is very rewarding to watch your child make new friends and develop social skills. At the same time, you need to be sensitive to your child's growing independence. Sooner or later, most kids tell their parents that they would rather the parents weren't *their* coach, leader, and so on. Don't let it upset you. In all likelihood, this means that you have done a great job and the child is ready to be a little more independent.

You can also help smooth your child's social development by being a good listener. From the earliest years, you need to have a regular time when your child feels comfortable confiding in you and talking about the day. Develop daily rituals that provide opportunities to talk from the heart. Activities that are particularly good for this are a few moments in the rocking chair every morning or evening, family dinners, bath time, or daily periods of medical therapy you do at home.

The discussions you have at these times will help your child recognize the difference between incidents that occur because of his disability and incidents that occur simply as part of growing up. You might share similar incidents from your youth to show how you handled them (or wish you had in retrospect).

If you hear things that make you angry, step back from your feelings for a minute. Does your child want you to handle it for him or just be a sounding board while he decides the best way to handle the situation? If you are not sure, ask.

When your child does want your help, what is the best way to give it? Should you intervene? Should you find resources to help your child handle it? Will your understanding, encouragement, and support be all your child needs to be able to handle the situation?

The key is to empower your child so he develops the skills to grow into the best person he is capable of being. The social skills he develops in community activities will provide a major boost to his self-confidence and ability to cope with the world.

Teaching Others to Meet Your Child's Needs

Over the years, you will have to teach others to meet your child's needs if he is to have any independence from you at all. If you do this successfully, your child will eventually start taking this task over for you.

Often, the skills you need to teach others will be relatively simple, such as:

- If your child uses a wheelchair, you may need to teach others how to "kick" the chair up over the front step so your child can get into his friends' homes to play.

- If your child has special dietary requirements, the parents of play-mates may be nervous about offering snacks. You can teach them what kinds of treats your child can enjoy with his friends.

- If your child has a seizure disorder, friends (and their parents) can be taught not to panic and how to handle those seizures.

- If your child has a hearing impairment and uses sign language, you may find that others (especially children) really enjoy learning signs so they can communicate with him.

Other needs can be pretty obvious. A child who has significant paralysis or is very spastic has needs that are easily noticed. In the early years, you or a parent substitute (like an aide at school) will have to do many routine services such as helping your child get out his lunch and possibly feeding it to him. Unless your child has a tendency to choke on his food, there is no reason why he (or his aide) cannot teach his friends and classmates how to get his lunch out—and possibly even help him eat it. That way, lunch breaks can really be shared with his friends and not be a time when he is alone with adults while classmate socialize.

At other times, the needs and skills will be more involved. When

10-year-old Maggie wanted more independence, the main obstacle was that she frequently needed to have secretions suctioned from her trach. Since she was quadriplegic, she couldn't do it for herself even though she could drive an electric wheelchair. After talking with the parents of several friends who had already shown a mature attitude, Maggie's mom taught several young friends how to do the suctioning. There were a lot of giggles about how gross it was—and some rather colorful names for the sound the suction machine made—but now Maggie can go to fast food restaurants with friends and go to their homes to play.

You need to evaluate your child's needs and the maturity of her friends before you teach them skills that will enable your child to have more freedom. Sometimes children may be eager to take on responsibilities that they are not quite ready for yet. In those situations, you may be able to allow them to assist your child, but only under adult supervision.

At all times you must keep your responsibility to others in mind. If you are thinking about teaching a minor skills that have a medical aspect, such as tracheal suctioning, you must talk with the parents of that minor and get their permission.

Caution: Never expect a child to exercise adult judgment in any situation and never expect an adult you train to react to an urgent situation the way you would. If you have any doubts at all about whether someone should be trained to meet your child's personal or medical needs, err on the side of caution. Your child's physician, therapists, and other medical professionals can advise you on the specifics of your child's situation.

Getting the Most Out of Life

Living life to the fullest is a goal we each strive for. What is it that you really want for yourself, your child, and your whole family? It is easy to think of the big-ticket items such as fancy vacations and expensive entertainment equipment, but it can be hard to make those dreams come true. You can achieve many of the same results by keeping an eye open for budget-friendly alternatives. For instance, if there is an amusement park, concert, play, or other event that your family would love to experience together, look for creative ways to do it. If your child's school is planning a field trip there, you can help set it up and be a chaperone. Disability-related organizations sometimes get a block of tickets at reduced costs or even free for support groups they sponsor. Organizations that sponsor events to benefit disability-related organizations occasionally donate tickets to their events to clients and their families. Get in touch with the patient-services coordinator to find out what opportunities may be available and ask what can be done to make the events you are interested in possible for you and for others.

On the other hand, you may find that by taking a few moments a day from activities you do not really care about you can find time for other things that do add to your quality of life. Reading story books from the library and feeding ducks at the park are fun, free pastimes you can all enjoy together. Turn off the television and go outside with a book to help you identify the constellations in the stars. Sing songs together. Play board games. (In my house everyone cheats at Yahtzee,® but we play Boggle® for blood. Be willing to adjust the rules so they work for your family.) Work together on jigsaw puzzles. Cook. Draw pictures. Act out favorite stories. And while you have certainly noticed that life has its share of thorns (and too often more than its share), don't forget to stop and smell the roses.

8

School Daze

Your Child's Educational Rights

Until 1975, children with disabilities faced unequal and often unfair situations when they sought an education. Depending on the whimsy of their local school district, they might get an appropriate education or they could find themselves offered little or no education in a "separate" program. Sometimes they were denied any services at all.

When P.L. 94-142, The Education for All Handicapped Children Act, was signed into law by President Gerald Ford, children between the ages of 6 and 18 became entitled to a wide range of educational services. Individual states were required to write laws and regulations that would conform to that federal law. By 1990, all states were required to provide services for children with disabilities beginning at age three.

Currently, most states provide services for children with disabilities from birth through age 21 (when necessary) under the renamed P.L. 94-142, now known as P.L. 101-476, The Individuals with Disabilities Education Act (IDEA).

Investigating Your Preschool Options

You now have several options when it comes to your child's preschool experience. The choice you make will be determined by the extent of your child's disability and your family's resources, preferences, and job commitments.

In addition to home care or day care, you have the option of enrolling your child in special programs through your local school district. Your child is not required to attend school until the age he or she would normally start. However, after checking out the available programs, you may decide that the special classes and therapies are a good reason to get an early start.

Beginning the Educational Process

We all know that knowledge is power. The more knowledge you have about your child's needs and legal rights, the better advocate you can be for him. So the first step in getting your child the best possible education is educating yourself.

Your state department of education has a department with a name like "Department of Special Education" that provides handbooks and other information about the special education process and programs. You can get the address and phone number from your local school district or your neighborhood library. Contact that office and have the publications sent to you. Then read them. They are usually written in a simple style that everyone can understand.

Every school system is required to have a set of regulations outlining and governing its special educational programs and services. Again, get a copy and read it.

Don't let yourself be turned off by the term *special education.* Too many people equate it with mental retardation and feel it has nothing to do with their child who is physically disabled (and who may actually be academically gifted). Depending on your child's personal needs, the "special" in his education may be a special bus that delivers him to your door, books printed in braille, help with toileting needs, an aide who can "sign" lessons that other students hear, or other supportive services. On the other hand, if your child needs a great deal of assistance—anything from a small, sheltered classroom to individualized academic assistance—that is available, too.

Once you decide to explore the available special services, you need to contact the school district and request an evaluation—even if your child is already in school and a progressive or accidental disability becomes a problem in the current educational setting.

Steps in the Process

Start by writing a letter to your school district's special education department requesting an evaluation (and keep a copy of it). In fact, you should keep copies of all documents and a record of every contact you have with school district personnel. (This includes notes on conversations you had by phone in the form of a telephone log or on-going diary of events.) In all likelihood, the process will go well. But if it doesn't, you will need this paper trail to prove what you have been trying to achieve.

Once you have written the letter asking for evaluation for special educational services (or filled out the form your district uses) and it has been received, the clock starts ticking. The school district has 60 days to complete the evaluation process, so be sure your letter or the form you sign has the current date on it and keep a copy for your records. Also, your child cannot be tested without your written consent, so this is not something you can handle over the phone.

The next step is to schedule a screening to determine if your child needs any services. If it is determined that your child does not require any services, you will be notified in writing. If you do not disagree, this is the end of the process and your child will not receive any services. Should you disagree, you may request a Level I Due Process Hearing (as described later in this chapter) to challenge that decision.

When it is determined that your child does require services, the next step is a Case Study Evaluation. During this evaluation, the district administers a series of diagnostic tests (for example social development, or vision/hearing) and gathers information and records to evaluate how your child's physical problems are affecting his educational progress. Your child must be evaluated by people who are fluent in his or her primary language or mode of communication. In fact, all communications about your child's educational needs

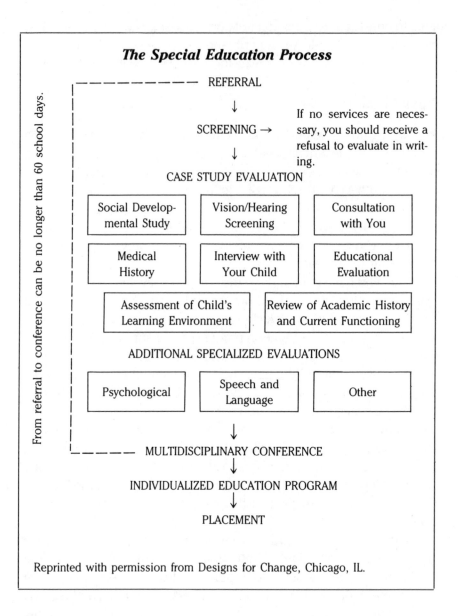

The Special Education Process

REFERRAL

↓

SCREENING → If no services are necessary, you should receive a refusal to evaluate in writing.

↓

CASE STUDY EVALUATION

Social Developmental Study	Vision/Hearing Screening	Consultation with You
Medical History	Interview with Your Child	Educational Evaluation

Assessment of Child's Learning Environment	Review of Academic History and Current Functioning

ADDITIONAL SPECIALIZED EVALUATIONS

Psychological	Speech and Language	Other

↓

MULTIDISCIPLINARY CONFERENCE

↓

INDIVIDUALIZED EDUCATION PROGRAM

↓

PLACEMENT

From referral to conference can be no longer than 60 school days.

Reprinted with permission from Designs for Change, Chicago, IL.

must be provided in your primary language and mode of communication.*

You will be consulted and asked a lot of questions about your child, from birth to the present. Keep the conversation focused on your child; don't digress to airing family problems that are not relevant. The interviewer may record them and your statements may come back to haunt you later. Do be prepared to talk about your child's strengths as well as his weaknesses so the evaluator(s) will get an accurate picture of his abilities. If your son has previous academic experience, the school district will need those records and will arrange to interview your child. You will need to give your permission for the tests and for the district to receive medical records from doctors and hospitals.

For its convenience, the district will often ask you to sign a permission form for medical records that amounts to a fishing license. It can be used to get any and all records the district can find.

There is an alternative to giving the school district the ability to have full access to all of your child's medical records. If you believe there are sensitive records that might be damaging to your child in any way or at any time if they got out—or if you believe there are inaccuracies in the records—do not sign the permission form. Confidentiality is a wonderful concept that normally works, but the records are handled by real people who sometimes make mistakes.

Tell district personnel that you will write a letter to the physician you want the district to deal with and ask her to write a letter to the district outlining your child's medical condition, results of applicable tests, medications currently being taken, and therapies currently being pursued, as well as prescriptions for any physical or occupational therapy that your child needs that can be provided through the district.

If the district personnel have other specific questions that are not answered by that letter, you can ask them for a list of those questions.

---

*If you are reading this book to assist families whose children are physically disabled and who are not fluent in English, you will want to notify them of the right to have all communications in their primary language. Bureaucracies might be tempted to skirt this requirement if they think family members are able to communicate somewhat in English even though they are not fluent in it.

If you agree they are reasonable, you can write another letter to the doctor requesting the answers to those specific questions. You may want to have a conversation with your doctor ahead of time outlining your family's views on privacy.

Once all the material has been gathered (and within 60 days from your initial request/referral), there will be a meeting to discuss the results. You can bring anyone you choose along with you and the Individualized Education Program (IEP) may be written at this meeting.

Understanding the Individualized Education Program (IEP)

The Individualized Education Program (IEP) is a document that sets out the educational goals for your child for the coming year and the services the school district will supply to assist your child in achieving those goals. This document must be completed and signed by you and the district before any services can be supplied to your child.

The meeting at which the IEP document is written must be held within 30 days after it is determined that your child is eligible for special education and/or related services and no more than 60 days from your initial referral. You will receive a written notice at least 10 days before the meeting is scheduled giving you the time, place, and a listing of who is expected to be there.

The people who normally attend the IEP meeting with you include your child (if you wish and/or when appropriate), someone from the school district who has the authority to commit the district to the services outlined in the IEP; your child's current teacher or, if your child is just starting school, a teacher of children who are the same age as yours, and other professionals who the district feels can help, such as a member of the evaluation team who can speak to the evaluation procedures and your child's results or district psychologists.

If it is more difficult to attend meetings at one time of day than another, it is a good idea to let the district know when you first request that your child be evaluated for special education and services. Because of the number of professionals the school district may want to bring to the meeting, it can be complicated and time consuming to find a time when everyone can get together. If you want the meeting scheduled for your convenience, you are more likely to be successful if you provide this information up front.

If it is simply not possible for you to attend the IEP meeting, the school district must attempt to get your input by other methods such as by phone calls or visits to your home or job.

You Are an Important Member of the IEP Team

Make every effort to have at least one parent (or parent substitute such as foster parent) at every IEP meeting. Your participation will enable you to advocate for your child and protect your child's interests. It is a lot easier to get the educational program right in the planning stages than it is to go back later and correct it. It is also a good idea to bring along a family member, friend, or advocate who can help you take notes during the meeting and serve as a sounding board later.*

You also have the option of bringing professionals with you to help support you and advocate for your child. You might consider including any social workers your family currently works with who can help you interface new educational plans with current programs you are involved with. You might want to bring patient service directors from disability organizations you deal with or therapists your child works with because these people can assist you in helping all members of the committee understand your child's unique needs. In the unlikely case that you suspect that the district is not going to be cooperative, you may choose to bring a lawyer (for legal counsel and/or negotiating skill), although this is not usually necessary.

It never hurts to bring a tape recorder along and place it on the table. When you start it, say the date of the meeting and ask everyone to introduce themselves when the tape is recording. This gives you a record of the meeting that you can listen to later to evaluate how

---

*If you are reading this book to assist a family that does not speak English as its primary language, the district is required to provide a translator at all meetings. Be sure to make your request for a translator to the district in writing at the earliest possible time in the process.

effective you were at advocating for your child or share with other relatives who were not at the meeting. In the unlikely case that the district is behaving inappropriately, you will have a record.

The Contents of the IEP

Your child's IEP must include specific information, beginning with a description of his current educational status. The IEP also includes the annual goals you and the committee set with measurable, short-term objectives to help meet those goals.

Your child's educational setting should be detailed, including how much time your child will spend in regular educational programs including academic, nonacademic, and extracurricular programs versus how much (if any) time will be spent in special day classes, with resource teachers, and other special settings.

Depending on your child's individual needs, the schooling may take place in one of the following settings:

- A regular or special education class of a public school with the appropriate related services.

- A special education program in a private school setting (that may be either a day or residential school).

- A special home or hospital program. (If you know that your child will miss more than two weeks of school for upcoming medical/ surgical reasons, call the school district as soon as you know to set up home/hospital schooling.)

- A special education program in a government-funded residential facility.

Related Services You Can Expect

Transportation is often high on the parents' list. This can be especially important if your child is not able to get to school on her own without becoming exhausted or if standing at a regular bus stop or walking to school in inclement weather would pose a health risk.

You may want to limit travel time in the IEP so that your child doesn't spend hours a day sitting on a bus while it drives around town picking up and dropping off other students.

If your child is trached and needs frequent suctioning or has another condition that requires closer supervision than the driver is likely to be able to offer, you may want to put a clause in the IEP requiring the school district to have a properly trained aide on the bus whenever your child is riding it.

Extended school year programs (summer school) should be available to your child if her disability has resulted in or is likely to result in regression during breaks in her educational program.

Adaptive physical education should be provided when appropriate. Consider the quality of the available program. You may be able to work with teachers (especially in the K–6 range) who will adapt their current program to include your child. For instance, one first-grade teacher adapted relay races so the students racing against a child in a wheelchair had to run backwards on that leg of the race. Only you can decide whether the program being offered is better for your child than participating in whatever way possible with her peers in a regular program.

If you want some extra support and information in creating a physical education program in your child's IEP, contact National Handicapped Sports, 451 Hungerford Drive, Suite 100, Rockville, MD 20850; (301)217-0960. This organization can give you specific information on designing an adaptive physical education program and ensuring that your child receives the program he is entitled to under federal law.

Does your child need support services? Does she need help with manipulating classroom materials? Does she need help with tasks involving handwriting or note taking? Does she need an interpreter? Psychological services? Physical and/or occupational therapy? Speech and language services? Assistance with toileting needs? Someone to help feed her at lunch or snack breaks? When these services are needed, the district is required to supply them.

Special adaptive equipment must be supplied by the school district if it is necessary for your child to participate in school. This could include a computer, a communication board, TDD devices for children who are deaf, adapted switches or controls for equipment your child will be expected to manipulate, or other technological devices suited to your child's individual needs. Think ahead to prepare for all eventualities. If your child shows an interest in participating in school plays or other activities that take place on a stage, the school should make that stage accessible even if that means installing a small elevator (there are even some relatively compact movable ones) or moving the play off the stage.

Once you have determined what adaptive equipment the school district will supply, find out whether the equipment is only to be available at school, or if you will be able to bring equipment (especially important things like communication devices) home for evenings, weekends, and vacations. You may be able to convince district personnel (perhaps with the help of your child's therapists) that her educational goals will be achieved more rapidly if the equipment can be used both at home and at school (and it may help keep you from having to write out her homework every night!). If this is what you need, include it in her IEP so that a teacher or administrator cannot unilaterally make a decision that would keep you from bringing the equipment home at some point in the future.

Once your child reaches high school age, you need to be especially aware of the provisions in her IEP for graduation and/or transition. Are you aiming for a regular academic diploma? Will she need help assessing different colleges for their programs and accessibility? Does your child need vocational training? Does she need training leading toward independent living? Whatever goals you are working toward, be sure they are included in the IEP and the steps necessary to achieve that goal are also listed and supported.

Preparing for IEP Meetings

You will have an IEP meeting before your child receives special services and at least annually from then on. Here are the steps you can take to make the meeting more successful:

Have a firm idea of what you expect your child to achieve and receive in the coming year. If your child needs related services such as physical, occupational, or speech therapy, or perhaps adaptive physical education, the IEP should state the number of minutes per week the services will be offered and where they will be offered. Ask what periods of the day these activities are scheduled to take place. For instance, you would not want your child to miss reading or math lessons every day so he can do adaptive physical education—even if it is more convenient for the P.E. teacher that way.

Know what your child needs. Ideally, the school district personnel will offer you all the resources and services that will be beneficial. Unfortunately, some school districts may try to minimize what they make available to children who have disabilities. This can make them less likely to offer special services (like adaptive physical education) or resources (like speech boards or books in Braille) unless you know exactly what your child needs to succeed in school and are willing to insist that he get it.

Bring advocates when needed. You have the right to bring people who you believe will help you understand the process, speak for your child in a way you cannot, or who will simply be there to protect your child's rights.

If you are confused by the language being used by the district and feel that you don't quite understand what is happening, it is absolutely appropriate and necessary to bring someone who is more experienced in dealing with these situations who can counsel you. Don't worry. Before long you will find you are able to handle it yourself as you learn more about the process.

If you feel you need extra support, consider bringing along a medical professional who is familiar with your child's situation. This could be a physician who can explain medical needs or a physical therapist who can offer suggestions about adapting physical educational activities to include your child.

In the event you feel the need for a legal advocate, you have the right to bring someone who is knowledgeable about your child's rights.

Be Alert to Protect Your Child's Interests

Sometimes what you want for your child and what the school district offers are not the same. If the school district wants you to believe that it should not offer a service you believe your child needs, someone may tell you that the district can't afford it or that it has never been done for anyone else. That's a cop out and you don't have to let the school district get away with it.

If the service is required under federal law, it is irrelevant whether your district has funded it before; it has to fund it now. If the district tries the guilt trip ("If we do this for your child, we can't fully fund the school library."), remember these three things:

1. The school district doesn't have a choice unless you provide it.

2. A few dollars spent to assist your child's special needs now will undoubtedly more than pay off by enabling his adult independence later.

3. It is the law and the district will find a way to finance it.

In your negotiations over the IEP or any other situation, it pays to start with a pleasant attitude. Remember the old saying that you can catch more flies with sugar than with vinegar? Still true.

The school district itself is not (usually) the enemy. It is made up of employees who are dealing with their own set of problems, including tight budgets, confusing regulations, grumpy bosses, and personal crises. If you acknowledge the employees as individuals and assure them that you understand their problems, you are likely to get them on your side.

One parent found that noticing and complementing the district personnel on some personal point (such as their garments) helps disarm them and makes the meeting go more smoothly. However, remember that you are not at the meeting to make friends, you are there to advocate for your child. Even if things get difficult, it is still your job to make sure your child gets the education and services he needs.

If Disagreements Arise: Making the IEP Process Work

Sometimes you get to the end of the IEP meeting and the school district personnel offer you a form outlining a school program or placement that you do not believe is in your child's best interest. Do not sign it if the form states that you agree with the placement.

However, you may sign a form that simply states you attended the meeting. Check your state's regulations to determine how disagreements at the IEP meeting are handled.

If you sign the IEP itself, you are agreeing to the terms it contains and it can take a great deal of time to get them changed later. You should only sign the IEP when you agree with all the terms it contains. Also remember, if your child's physical or educational situation changes before the time you would normally negotiate another IEP, you have the right to call for a meeting to revise the current one.

If you disagree with your child's proposed IEP (perhaps it calls for a sheltered classroom and you want him mainstreamed or it does not include provisions for the speech therapy he needs) or you find yourself dissatisfied with the way his current IEP is being administered—or suspect that your child has been denied his legal rights—you have the right to file a complaint with your state board of education, request mediation, and/or call for an impartial due process hearing.

Filing a Complaint

The *complaint* is a first step when you believe the actions of the school district are not complying with the law. You should write a letter to the state board of education outlining the violations you are alleging and requesting an investigation. Be sure to include your child's name and the name of his school and school district as well as your name, address, and a daytime phone where you can be reached.

Mediation can be requested by you or by the school district when you cannot settle your differences. You (and the school district) may not be permitted to tape record the meeting since it is created to be a forum for clarifying the issues and working out an agreement and is nonbinding on both parties.

Due process is the most formal step you can take before filing a civil lawsuit. You should consider initiating due process procedures when your school district either refuses to provide a free, appropriate public education or refuses to change your child's educational placement when you believe it is warranted.

You need to request a Level I Impartial Due Process Hearing when all other efforts have been unsuccessful. Start by writing a letter requesting the hearing to the superintendent of your local school district. The hearing must be scheduled by the district at a time that is convenient to both you and the district as well as representatives you may choose to bring to support your case (i.e., physicians, therapists, social workers, attorneys, and so on).

The hearing officer who chairs the meeting is sometimes appointed by the state board of education. She may be an educator or other person who has a broad background in special education laws. This hearing officer cannot be an employee of an agency involved with education or have a personal or professional interest in the outcome of the hearing. Within 10 days of your hearing, the officer will send you her recommendations by certified mail.

Types of Disputes Settled Through Due Process. The kinds of disagreements that are frequently settled through the use of due process include:

- The specific kind of placement your child needs (i.e., fully or partially mainstreamed in public school, placement in a private school at public expense).
- The kinds of related services your child should receive including occupational therapy, speech therapy, and/or physical therapy.
- Disputes about whether your child is receiving the program you have previously outlined in an IEP.

Disputes Not Likely to Be Settled Through Due Process. Certain kinds of disputes do not tend to be settled through the due process procedure. They are primarily attitude problems that you may not be able to force people to correct. These kinds of problems include:

- Disagreeable attitudes of school personnel.
- Delaying handling your concerns until the last legal moment.
- Disregard of your personal choices such as your preference for one teacher over another when both have appropriate qualifications.

If you find yourself facing problems like these three, you may not have any administrative recourse as long as the school district obeys the letter of the law. However, you might consider consulting a psychological therapist to help you develop skills to build a more cooperative relationship with the people who are employed by the district.

When You Are Not Satisfied Through Due Process

What if you have completed the Level I Due Process and still are not satisfied with the outcome? When you feel that the correct decision has not been reached, you may request a Level II review decision. If you are still unsatisfied with the Level II decision, you can consult a lawyer to see if you should file a civil lawsuit.

If you try to skip ahead to file the lawsuit without going through due process, the judge may just order you to go back and try the remedy of due process before you can have a court hearing. Going through the full process also shows that you tried to do everything you could to work with the district and can support your case.

How to Evaluate School Placement Options

Your child is entitled to receive a free, appropriate public education in the least restrictive environment she can benefit from. Most students who have physical disabilities attend public schools where they participate in regular education classes as well as extracurricular activities. You should only consider allowing your child to be schooled in an alternative program or setting when her individual needs cannot be accommodated within the regular school setting.

That does not mean that your child should go to a special, sheltered school just because it has accessible bathrooms or is built in one story. If your child is capable of benefiting from regular schools, it is the district's responsibility to remove architectural barriers that would keep your child from attending.

As soon as is practical *before* your child starts school or moves up to the next level school, you should plan to visit the campus. Call ahead and ask the principal when would be a convenient time and whether he can arrange for you to sit in and observe some classes (especially at the younger levels). Some of the areas you should pay special attention to when you are evaluating how the facility will serve your child include the:

- Lunch room
- Bathroom
- Auditorium
- Playground
- Nurse's office

What changes, if any, will need to be made?

If you are in an area where you have a neighborhood school but the district suggests another school nearby, visit both and consider the educational standards of both schools, the staff attitudes, and the other points the district brings up. Add to the equation the opportunity (or lack thereof) for your child to participate in extracurricular activities at the different sites as well as the potential difficulties of getting together with friends to play if they live too far away. Also, keep in mind the potential benefits of having all your children at the same school.

If your child's IEP requires special services (such as physical therapy), the district may tell you that she should go to a school across town because that is where the therapy room is. If you prefer that she goes to your neighborhood school and there is no other major reason why she shouldn't, consider putting a requirement in the IEP that she be bused to therapy after her regular school day and bused home after therapy is over. If your child's disability requires some substantial time in special classes that are only offered on one site, you may not have the same amount of flexibility.

Verify That the IEP Is Being Adhered To

Even the best IEP is worthless if the provisions in it are not carried out. Plan to keep in touch with the school personnel from time to time to verify that the goals and services outlined in your child's IEP are being adhered to.

One way to keep an eye on this is to volunteer at the school. Choose an activity you are comfortable with whether it is tutoring in the classroom or serving as an officer in the Parents' Club. This will give you personal insight into the strengths and weaknesses of your child's school and its staff as well as knowledge of the way day-to-day concerns are handled.

Being involved in your child's school is also a way of keeping the school aware of his individual needs. For instance, if they are planning to renovate the playgrounds, you can keep the design committee aware of ways the playground can assist in integrating disabled and able-bodied students for recreation and socialization.

If You Are Going to Move

Once you have determined the area you are moving to, contact school districts in the communities you are considering living in and ask for information about their schools and current programs. Before you purchase or rent a home, visit the schools that sound best and pick the one or ones you feel will best serve your child. Then, find a home in that attendance area if possible. It will simplify your life and your child's immeasurably. Also, be sure to bring a copy of your child's current IEP and school records when you meet with personnel at the new school.

When to Change Your Child's Program

If your child's education is progressing well, you probably don't need to even think about changing her program. On the other hand, if she is in a special day class or is taken out of her regular class for special services and you suspect that she is not getting the best possible education, there may come a time when you will want to consider some changes.

Changing a program will require a new IEP, but before you call for a new IEP meeting (see page 114), there is some homework you should do. Ask yourself if the current problem can be handled simply. Some serious problems that deserve your attention include:

- Is your child falling behind in math or reading because she is being pulled out of class for things like occupational therapy? Perhaps you can work with the therapist and teacher to set up a better schedule.

- Has your child reached a point where you feel that the potential benefit of the physical therapy she is receiving does not offset the value of the social contact she misses when she has therapy instead of recess? Before you call an IEP meeting, talk with your child's physician about whether the therapy is still beneficial or whether you could be trained to do it at home (when it would be less likely to interfere with her social development). Consider calling her current therapist and see if the therapy schedule could be changed (maybe to before or after school).

- Are your child's IEP goals being met? If the teacher is acting more like a babysitter, it might be time to move to another class.

- Does your child feel safe at school? There is a normal amount of roughhousing in any school, but every child has a right to feel safe. Document the problem (such as dates she was hit on the playground) and talk with the administration. If they cannot or will not protect your child from danger, demand a transfer to another classroom or campus.

When Your Efforts to Compromise Fail

If you are not able to get satisfaction in correcting problems with your child's placement, contact your school district and call an IEP meeting to make the necessary changes. Be sure you have a more concrete reason than just that you don't like the teacher. Document the reason(s) why you want your child's program changed and have a firm idea of exactly what you want.

If you do not get satisfaction through the IEP process, you have the same options outlined earlier in this chapter for disagreements over the content or execution of the IEP.

Your Legal Rights

Getting your child the education he deserves can be challenging under the best of conditions. A disability adds a layer of complication but it also offers a layer of legal protection.

This chapter only provides an overview of what is available to you. Your child has specific rights under federal and state laws and those rights are constantly being refined. If you have any questions, contact your state department of special education, your school district, or local advocacy groups.

You might also read the book, *Negotiating the Special Education Maze: A Guide for Parents and Teachers* (Woodbine House, 1990, $14.95), by Winifred Anderson, Stephen Chitwood, and Deidre Hayden. This book is a comprehensive resource that will give you detailed information about every step of the educational process you will face with your child.

Designs For Change is an organization in Chicago that works to educate parents of children who have disabilities so they can advocate effectively for their children in the school setting. One of the materials they have developed is a listing of the rights parents have to assure their child gets the best possible education (see box).

You Have the Right . . .

- To inspect, review, and obtain copies of your child's records.
- To have your child's records explained to you.
- To have all information written—that includes all letters and forms so that you can understand them. An interpreter must be provided if you need one.
- To be given 10 days' notice before the school changes (or refuses to change) the identification, evaluation, or placement of your child.
- To give consent before an evaluation or placement is made.
- To say no or revoke your consent.
- To have a case study evaluation completed within 60 school days. More than one criterion must be used for placement.
- To have a reevaluation done every three years or sooner if requested.
- To have an independent evaluation done and to have that evaluation considered when placement and program decisions are made.
- To have your child educated to the fullest extent possible with nondisabled peers, and to have your child removed from the regular education environment after supplementary aids and services being tried were not enough.

(Continued)

(Continued)

- To have your child participate with nondisabled children in nonacademic and extracurricular services and activities.
- To file a complaint with the state department of special education and have a report of findings within 60 days.
- To request an impartial due process hearing and to be informed of the procedures and any available free or low-cost legal service.

Reprinted with permission from Designs for Change.

For more specific information, consider contacting these resources:

U.S. Department of Education
TAPP (Technical Assistance for Parent Programs) Project
400 Maryland Ave., S.W.
Washington, D.C. 20202
Phone: (202)205-9032
Fax: (202)205-8105

Judy Heumann, Assistant Secretary
Office of Special Education Rehabilitative Services
400 Maryland Ave., S.W.
Washington, D.C. 20202
Phone: (202)205-5465
Fax: (202)205-9252

Office of Special Education Programs
400 Maryland Ave., S.W.
Washington, D.C. 20202
Phone: (202)205-5507
Fax: (202)205-9070

9

Keeping Good Records

School Records

You have the absolute right to review your child's school records and obtain a copy of them. You also have the right to have these records explained to you. No one outside your child's school or program can gain access to those records unless you give them written permission.

Occasionally, you can get access to these records by simply asking at the school office. Frequently, you will have to write a letter the district can keep for its records. Send the letter by mail, return receipt requested, so you will have documentation of the date it was received. Here is a sample letter:

Date
Your return address
Your phone number

Principal _____
Name of School
Address of School

Dear Principal _____,

As I am entitled to under law, I am requesting the opportunity to review (or receive copies of) my child's temporary and permanent school records. I understand that these records should be made available to me within 15 school days of this request. Please notify me using the phone number or address above as soon as the records are available.

I appreciate your prompt attention to this matter.

Sincerely,

Your Name

Your Home Files

Copies of the school records are only one part of a file you should be keeping at home. This file will be enormously helpful when you need to get your child into special education, move from one school to another, deal with social service agencies, or even meet with new medical professionals.

Following is a list of records you should be keeping together in your home for easy reference. It is helpful to purchase an accordion-type file that has separate pockets you can label. In addition to organizing a great deal of paperwork, they are portable enough for you to carry to meetings.

The home file of your child's records should include:

1. *A certified copy of the birth certificate.* Keep the original in a safety deposit box.
2. *Medical records.* Include a copy of the letters from your physician supporting your request for special education or other services, immunization records, medication records (including allergies), and so on.
3. *School records.* Include previous IEPs, report cards, letters to and from the school district, relevant notes from teachers, and notations about awards or recognitions.
4. *Evaluations.* Include evaluations of your child's needs for physical, occupational, speech/language, or other therapies as well as psychological testing. Some of these evaluations may have been done by school personnel; others may have been done by your medical providers or others recommended by them.

5. *Communication records.* These could be something that you put in the file only after the fact or when you are expecting to go to a meeting. You might include things like the notebook you send to school with your child every day where you and the teacher note anything going on that you believe the other should know. It is also a place to put notes about any conversations you have with the school district or social service agencies. You might also keep a notebook by the phone and keep a record of the date and subject of telephone conversations you have with personnel from the school district or social service agencies.

6. *Social service agency information.* File records specific to any social service agencies you deal with (for instance, an agency that supplies respite care). If you are dealing with some very regularly, give each its own file.

7. *Future reference.* Save fliers, notes, and other information you pick up about organizations and resources that you don't need just yet but that might be helpful in the future or to share with others you know. Otherwise, these gems tend to get misplaced and you can never find them when you need them.

8. *Medical equipment suppliers.* Record the names of suppliers and copies of the purchase orders for any medical equipment in one file. Then, if you ever need a replacement part, you know where to find the information you need to order it—and maybe even find it's still under warranty!

9. *Bragging rights.* Keep a few samples of your child's best school work, best art work, and records of other accomplishments here. This material can be very helpful when dealing with bureaucrats who need to be reminded that your child is not just a set of problems; he is also a loved human being with talents and gifts just like any other child.

10. *Your guess.* What else is unique to your situation that either people keep asking to see or you keep wanting to show them?

10

Choosing Medical Equipment and Suppliers

Welcome to the fascinating world of medical equipment. It can be the most frustrating aspect of dealing with your child's disability. At the same time, equipment offers the amazing ability to enhance (or even create) your child's ability to function in his world. Sometimes it may even make it possible for your child to continue living at all.

Much of the equipment your child needs is obvious: a wheelchair or walker for someone with an orthopedic disability, hearing aids, glasses, syringes, and so on. There also may be marvelously helpful equipment you will hear about through medical professionals or other parents that you may never have thought of.

Purchasing Equipment

You might think that the first thing to consider is your child's physical needs and the type of equipment that is most likely to be helpful. Sort of.

Actually, before you are ready to order that first piece of hardware, you better spend some time figuring out how you are going to pay for it. Medical equipment is expensive and most insurance plans and social programs have very specific steps you need to follow if they are going to pay for part or all the equipment costs. If you think you can order the equipment first and be reimbursed later, you may be very seriously disappointed. Always check with your insurance company or the social program you think will pay the bills before you place orders for equipment you cannot afford to pay for yourself.

Requesting Payment from Your Insurance Carrier

If you have medical insurance or are covered under a government program like Medicaid, check with your benefits counselor about what expenses will be covered and what has to be done to get those benefits. Frequently, you will be expected to get a prescription for the equipment from a medical doctor and there may be some restrictions on which suppliers you can use. You also may be responsible for obtaining whatever documentation the insurance company wants to justify the equipment that is being requested.

What to Do If Your Request Is Denied

If your initial request for funding to purchase equipment under your insurance policy is denied, consider filing an appeal. Your client advocate or benefits counselor should be able to tell you how to file that appeal and what documentation you should bring with you. In the event you feel that your claim is being unjustly denied, contact your insurer and file an appeal. If that fails, you might want to consider contacting the insurance commissioner for your state to file a complaint. (The number is available from the phone operator in your state capital or by calling the office of a state legislator.)

If you do not have insurance—or if the insurance you have will not cover enough of the expense—talk with the social worker at your hospital and the patient service coordinator at any disability organizations you have contact with. They may be aware of special programs in your state for disabled children, funds available through the disability organization, and other resources.

For instance, local service clubs often help families whose children have disabilities acquire needed equipment. They also may have the advantage of covering expense for things like travel costs and lodging for medical appointments and/or trips to acquire equipment when no one else will help with these expenses.

Sometimes, these local service clubs want some recognition of their gift, often by having the recipient come to a meeting for a presentation. Some families are not comfortable with this kind of attention; others choose to see it as neighbors helping neighbors. If this is a concern for you, before you accept assistance from an organization, ask them what, if anything, they will expect from you. Only you can decide how you feel about any cooperation they might hope for.

A Generous Helping Hand

There is a remarkable resource to consider for your child. The 22 Shriners Hospitals throughout the United States, Canada, and Mexico offer a full range of services for children who need medical care for orthopedic disabilities, spinal cord injuries, or serious burns. (Their programs are described fully in chapter 4). Patients at Shriners Hospitals get state-of-the-art equipment and prosthetic devices at no cost to the family.

Tracy was an active, happy preschooler who had no left hand and whose left arm only went to the elbow. As she grew and became more active, she began to notice that other kids had two hands and that having two hands was pretty useful. Tracy asked her mom about getting another hand like her friends.

The bad news was that the prosthesis Tracy needed was going to be expensive. Deeply saddened by the financial situation that threatened to keep her daughter from getting the second hand she so dearly wanted, the mom explained her problem to the orthotist. Fortunately, the shop knew about the wonderful work the Shriners did and referred the family to a local Shriners hospital. Now Tracy has a prosthetic lower arm and hand that enable her to grip and release objects and play with toys like her friends. The cost of the current prosthesis (roughly $10,000) and future prosthetic appliances as she grows are all covered completely by Shriners as are the therapy sessions Tracy needs to learn how to best use her new "hand."

Wherever you get the funding for the equipment your child needs, be sure to ask the funding source and the equipment supplier about how the costs for repairs and parts replacements are to be paid for. These expenses can add up surprisingly quickly even if you are very careful with the equipment.

Some Equipment Helps You, Too

Don't overlook the importance of equipment that will help you preserve your own health and ability to care for your child. Too often, parents and caregivers damage their health (especially their backs) before they look for mechanical assistance with childcare. There are hoists to lift a heavy child and help get him down the hall to the bathroom. There are special lifts to help you lift a wheelchair into a van or car trunk. Start looking for them (and ways to pay for them since they may not be covered by insurance) as soon as your child starts feeling a little heavy or you are considering purchase of a wheelchair or other heavy equipment. You won't be much help to your child if you don't take care of your own health.

Finding a Supplier

Whether you are looking for mechanical hardware such as electric wheelchairs and hoists or more intimate hardware such as braces and hearing aids, you need to shop for a supplier much the same way you shop for a good doctor.

Unless you are restricted to one supplier by the insurance company or organization that is paying the bills, start by asking for referrals from doctors, therapists, and especially families. The families are the most likely to know if the supplier really works closely with the family and the child to address all of their concerns.

For example, wheelchairs break down. Unfortunately, not everyone who sells wheelchairs is going to be able to give you fast service. Imagine if your "legs" had to go to the shop for a week or more! Also, body braces and other personal hardware may require several fittings before they are both comfortable and functional (as well as need adjustments as your child grows). A brace won't do your child any good if it is sitting in the closet because it was rubbing his skin raw.

Tips for Finding Suppliers

Do the following when you are looking for suppliers:

- Take time to meet the suppliers you are interested in working with.
- Visit their shop or store.

- See or try out the kinds of equipment they would be getting for your child.

- Ask questions about the equipment you are currently considering and what they would suggest.

One orthotist (brace maker) was working with a child who had scoliosis as a result of overall muscle weakness. While the child needed a corset-type brace that supported the trunk all around, the orthotist realized that the one-piece unit often constructed to assist with this condition would be a problem to get on and off. He designed a two-piece corset with adjustable velcro fastenings and even drilled small ventilation holes in the plastic to help maintain the child's skin condition in hot weather.

Look for a supplier, like that one, who sees your child as an individual and responds to her unique needs—not someone who sees selling medical supplies as a cookie-cutter process. There are a variety of potential solutions to almost any problem you and your child are facing—from hearing deficits to urinary incontinence to orthopedic shoe treatments. Take time to find the supplier and product that will work best for you before you take delivery. Once you have accepted a product or device, there may be a specified time that has to pass before you are entitled to replace the piece of equipment with a similar one and have it covered under your plan.

Choosing Equipment

When you are looking at buying or renting medical equipment, be sure to take your child's preference and style into account. This equipment will be with him all the time and becomes just as much a fashion accessory as a medical device.

Wheelchairs and other equipment can be ordered in a fantastic variety of colors. Just be sure to pick one that will look good with your child's skin tone (and it helps if it doesn't clash with every color in your child's wardrobe). Following are some other things to think about:

- *Consider overall visual impression.* This can be a tough call, but whenever possible, you want people to notice your child first and the hardware later. One key area here is the scale of the piece. Getting a "too large" wheelchair so he can grow into it will overwhelm him visually and may result in positioning problems.

- *If your child is old enough to talk, ask what he or she prefers* (especially on small, easily lost objects). A child who feels he had a part in choosing anything from eyeglass frames to hearing aids to crutches is much less likely to accidentally lose them than someone who hates their devices and wishes they would disappear.

- *Work with what you have.* A backpack featuring your child's favorite super hero hung on the handles of a wheelchair makes it look less threatening. If your child has a tracheostomy appliance, there is no law that says you have to use the plain white cord hospitals use to tie the appliance on. Grossgrain ribbon comes in beautiful colors and prints and is inexpensive enough to use new ones every trach change. *WARNING: Do not use ribbons that have metallic threads to hold on a trach appliance because the metal threads will irritate tender neck skin.*

- *Use your imagination.* Does your son need grab bars in the bathroom and you hate the idea of those institutional metal bars? Get in touch with a sailboat equipment supplier. The teak rails and bars used on boats will stand up to heavy, wet use and make a decorating statement at the same time. If your short-statured child needs a step stool to get in and out of bed, how about painting it to coordinate with the bed covers?

- *Think through exactly what you want out of equipment.* You may come up with surprising ways to achieve your functional goals and still have it be aesthetically pleasing.

- *How long will it take to receive the equipment?* Work with your supplier on this one. Some companies get orders out substantially faster than others. It is the same with spare parts. One program that made specially molded seats for young children routinely took so long to get the chairs finished that parents often found their children had already started outgrowing the chair before it even arrived.

11

Planning for Emergencies

By definition, an emergency is "a sudden, generally unexpected occurrence or set of circumstances demanding immediate action" *(Webster's New World Dictionary)*. You have undoubtedly begun to become accustomed to the idea that the unexpected occurrence is normal. Now you need to prepare for it. There are two levels of emergencies you need to anticipate in your planning.

Day-to-Day Situations

These situations include back-up plans if you do not meet the school bus in the afternoon. What would you do (and what would happen to your child) if you were delayed by a flat tire? Consider the different situations in your life that could cause you to be delayed in getting back to your child. Talk with the people who have your child and ask what their contingency plans call for; you might be surprised—not always pleasantly. One school district's contingency plan for when the parent did not meet the bus and could not be reached by phone was to drop the child at the police station or have her taken to juvenile hall until the parent could be found and could pick up the child. You can imagine what an incentive it was to get home on time!

You must also involve your child in planning for all types of situations that might arise. What other kinds of situations might your child find herself in that could become problems? What have you done to prepare your child to handle the situation herself? What have you done to provide back-up?

Do some role playing with her about what to do if a strange adult approaches her on the street or playground. Does she know neighbors who are likely to be home if she needs help? Can she use the phone or TDD or call for emergency assistance? Does she know her own phone number (including area code) so she can call home if she needs to?

Natural—and Unnatural—Disasters

There are major emergencies you cannot hope to control but which you can prepare for. In recent years, different parts of the United States have dealt with hurricanes, floods, riots, and earthquakes that have made it impossible for people to get clean water, electricity, and normal medical care. You owe it to your child and yourself to prepare for the possibility (no matter how remote it seems) that you might not have the things you currently take for granted.

What should you do?

Never get down to less than a week's supply of any medication your child (or anyone in your home) needs. If you put some aside in an emergency kit, be sure to replace it with fresh medication no less than two times a year (or more often if the medication expires more quickly). Remind yourself by checking your emergency kit when you change your clocks to and from daylight savings time. (Be sure to change the batteries in your smoke detector at the same time.)

Always keep fresh batteries on hand. If your child uses a hearing aid or other device that uses batteries, keep a fresh set with the medications. Also include fresh batteries for flashlights and portable radios.

Be prepared to maintain life-support equipment. If your child uses oxygen, talk to your supplier about how to insure that your child has an ample supply and how much you should keep at home. Does your child use equipment that requires electricity?

Check with your power company to determine its policy in an emergency situation. (They may tell you to take your child to the hospital in an emergency, but the roads may not be passable and the hospital itself may be damaged or overwhelmed with critical cases.) Consider whether you should have a small generator to run your child's critical equipment (or to keep the refrigerator going to keep medications fresh and potent).

Have a family disaster plan. Disasters don't always happen when you are all home together. Work out a family plan for what each person should do to get you all back together as quickly as possible. You might tell your school-age children that if a disaster happens on a school day, they should stay at school until you pick them up. For older children who are out and about more, you might have a short list of places you will look for them starting with school, your home, and maybe a third site where they are likely to find help, such as a church in the neighborhood. Otherwise, you will all run around aimlessly, worried and unable to find each other.

Many disasters, such as tornadoes, floods, and earthquakes, can make your home unliveable and stop supplies of safe water and food. Take a moment and contact your local police; they will be able to refer you to organizations that can give you information about the emergency preparations they recommend in your area. Then make the preparations they recommend.

Following is a chart to help you organize your preparations for emergencies. Hopefully, you will never need to use these items, but they could make all the difference if you need them. Photocopy the chart, fill it out, and keep it with your supplies.

Emergency Preparedness Checklist

MEDICATION	*Expiration Date*	*Amount on Hand*
_____	_____	_____
_____	_____	_____
_____	_____	_____
_____	_____	_____

BATTERIES	*Expiration Date*	*Size/Type*
_____	_____	_____
_____	_____	_____
_____	_____	_____

SAFETY EQUIPMENT   *Check If Included*

Flashlight(s)   _____   Portable Radio   _____

First Aid Kit   _____   Blankets (1 each)   _____

Potable Water   _____   Matches   _____
(Minimum 1 gallon/
person)

Canned/Dry Food   _____   Charcoal (to cook food _____
                                       in freezer)

Wrench (to turn off main gas line if necessary)   _____

LIFE SUPPORT

If there is no electricity, I will _____

_____

If the oxygen supplier cannot deliver, I will _____

_____

My other special concern is _____
In a disaster situation, I will handle it by _____

_____

12

Handling Your Child's Hospitalizations

Preparing Ahead of Time

From time to time, your child may require hospitalization for diagnosis, surgery, or other medical procedures. If you know in advance that you will be facing a hospitalization, your doctor should be able to arrange for you (and your child if he is old enough to understand what is going on) to visit the facility.

Many hospitals have special tours you and your child can take to familiarize yourselves with the facility. Others may have employees who will show you around personally. Ask. The more you know about the facility, its procedures, and its people, the better you will be able to handle the stress of hospitalization.

Spend as Much Time as Possible with Your Child

One of the great gifts you can give your children is simply being there with them when times are tough. A hug, a kiss, even just holding their hand can help them deal with medical procedures that you would give anything to protect them from.

If you can't be there, someone else your child cares about should be with him as much as possible during hospitalization and outpatient tests. This might be your spouse/partner, grandparents, aunts/uncles, family friends, or others who are close to him.

Please do not feel that you are the only one who can be there, especially if you have other children at home, a job, or other com- mitments. You also need to take a break from time to time even if it is only to get off the floor for a hot meal every day. Remember that after the hospitalization there will still be a recuperation time at home. If you have exhausted yourself in the hospital, you won't have any energy and comfort to offer your child after homecoming.

Also, consider your own physical and psychological limits. Some parents are able to handle being with their child through painful tests and others can't.

Recognize your own feelings and honor them. If you are able to keep your cool and focus solely on your child's needs, medical professionals will often welcome your support. If you know (or find out during the procedure) that you can't handle it, that is OK too. The doctors, nurses, and technicians are trained to work with patients and may be better able to comfort your child than you if you are too upset. In any case, you (or your spouse) can be there afterwards with hugs and kisses to help wipe the tears away.

Steps You Can Take to Help Staff See Your Child as You Do

Tack up some photos showing your child's personality and nor- mal life over the bed. Remember that the professionals you meet in the hospital are people too. When your child is feeling poorly or can't talk for himself, the photos can help hospital staff realize the kind of lifestyle they are working to return your child to.

Bring a favorite "lovie" from home. This could be a favorite stuffed animal, pillow, or anything that will make your child feel more comfortable. Also hang get-well cards around the room to personalize it and help your child feel loved and at home.

When allowed, dress your child in PJs from home. She will feel more comfortable than in hospital-issue gowns. Plan to have enough sets on hand to allow you to change her at least once a day.

Share your feelings with the staff. If your child's diagnosis often has a negative outcome, it is helpful to share literature with the staff that reflects your optimistic outlook.

One child I knew with a diagnosis that was frequently fatal was in the hospital for a lung infection. Her family saw this hospitalization as a temporary stumbling block, but the staff seemed to think she was in imminent danger of dying. Her family had researched the condition at the library of the local medical school and found articles that suggested that some children with this diagnosis did much better than expected.

In frustration, the parents made a stack of photocopies of the most optimistic articles and brought them into the hospital. They quietly placed them on the nurses' station and the copies disappeared over the next day.

Not surprisingly, once they understood that the girl was not necessarily on death's door, the staff's attitude became warmer and more positive which was helpful to both the child and the mother.

It takes a remarkable amount of energy for hospital staff to keep up to date on all the different medical conditions they treat. If you can help them access new information in a nonthreatening way, they are usually very grateful.

Know Your Parental Rights

Many hospitals have adopted the Bill of Rights for Parents which was developed by the Association for the Care of Children's Health (ACCH) to help families understand the ways staff is prepared to help make your child's hospitalization as positive as possible. ACCH's mission is to ensure that all aspects of children's health care are family centered, psychosocially sound, and developmentally appropriate. Even hospitals that have not adopted this particular set of rights probably have a similar document that sets out the rights that patients and their families can expect at that facility.

Parents' Bill of Rights

You and your child have a right to:

- *Respect and personal dignity.* You and your child will be treated with courtesy and respect. Medical professionals will introduce them-
(Continued)

(Continued)

selves and explain their role in your child's care. Your privacy and confidences will be respected and staff will take the time to listen to you and get to know your child.

- *Care that supports you as a family.* You can choose to stay with your child during most medical treatments. Hospital staff will provide a place for at least one family member to spend the night near your child.

- *Information you can understand.* You have the right to complete information from people helping you care for your child. You can ask what is happening to your child and why. Everything will be explained to you honestly, in ways you can understand. Someone who speaks your language will help explain things to you. You have the right to ask questions about anything that is unclear to you. If you choose, you can have a family member or other supportive person with you when hospital staff members are explaining things to you. You have the right to know about your child's condition and treatment plan and can review your child's medical records with health care personnel. The hospital should make a detailed listing of your child's hospital bill available to both your insurance carrier and you when you request it. You have the right to know the policies, procedures, and routines of the hospital where your child is a patient. You also have the right to know about the hospital's process for taking care of your concerns or complaints.

- *Quality health care.* You have a right to know who all the people are who care for your child in the hospital as well as what those people do. Medical personnel who work with your child should be experienced in caring for children his age. Your observations will be important in evaluating your child's condition and should be shared with and respected by medical staff. You have the right to know about all the treatment options being suggested for your child and whether those treatments are considered experimental or educational. When the treatment options are considered experimental or educational, you have the right to refuse treatment and be assured that staff will continue to take good care of your child. Also, before your child leaves the hospital, staff will teach you the medical techniques you need to know to properly care for your child as well as tell you about what people and places in your community will be available to help you.

- *Emotional support.* When your child is hospitalized, you can talk with health professionals about your feelings, questions, problems,

(Continued)

(Continued)

or concerns, and those professionals will listen to you and respect your feelings. You have the right to decide who you want to assist your family. If you want, hospital staff will help you meet other families who have had experiences like yours.

- *Care that respects your child's growth and development.* Hospital staff will consider all of your child's interests and needs, not just those related to his illness or disability. Your child will be cared for by people who understand the needs of children his age and who will try to keep his activities and schedule as normal as possible.

- *Make decisions about your child's care.* You have the right to any information you need to make decisions about your child's care. Hospital personnel will work in partnership with you and will explain all options so that you can understand the risks and know what the choices are for your child's care. You can ask for a second opinion from another doctor or for a consultation from a specialist. Within legal limits, you have the right to refuse treatments that have been recommended for your child. You can ask to change hospitals, and if that is possible, staff will facilitate the move. If it is necessary to move your child to another hospital, staff will make every effort not to move him until you have been told why.

Adapted with permission of the Association for the Care of Children's Health from *A Pediatric Bill of Rights.* The complete ACCH Bill of Rights includes rights for Children and Teens in addition to Parent's Rights. You can receive an entire set of these rights by contacting ACCH at 7910 Woodmont Ave., Suite 300, Bethesda, MD 20814 or calling (301) 654-6549. There may be a minimal fee for processing your request.

Strategies for Working with Hospital Staff

For the most part, people who work in hospitals are caring, supportive professionals who are doing their very best to help your child. If you work with them as equals and learn what they have to teach you about managing your child's medical condition you will often develop a warm, cooperative relationship that can go on for years.

Building a Relationship with Hospital Staff

First, keep your focus on what is best for your child. Remember that you are there to support and advocate for your child. As hard as it is, try to keep your feelings in check (unless you are talking with a therapist, a professional who has asked how you are doing, or sometimes another parent).

Second, welcome those who are supportive as members of your network. They can be helpful not only during the hospitalization(s) but possibly later for referrals and technical information. You can respect their professionalism while still firmly representing your child's needs and, when necessary, your family's decisions about the quality and quantity of health care he receives.

Third, be knowledgeable about your child's condition. You cannot be an effective advocate if you do not have your facts straight. Ask doctors, nurses, therapists, and other medical professionals to explain their diagnosis and treatment options. Ask diagnosis-specific organizations for their literature. Consider spending an afternoon in the library of a local medical school researching your child's diagnosis or review current literature on-line through a computer service (See Appendix 2).

What to Do if Things Don't Go Smoothly

While you are working hard at developing good relationships, remember that there may be times when it doesn't work. Before you decide to do anything about it, take a moment to think about whether you are really upset with that person or with what is happening to your child. When you have that answer, you are ready to act.

If You Are Having Trouble with Staff. If you are having trouble with a staff person, talk to your physician and/or that person's supervisor. Sometimes it is not possible or practical to talk with those people directly. In that case, go talk with the hospital ombudsman or the social worker who handles the ward your child is in. State your concern clearly and know what you want changed. Perhaps the offending person just needs some education, or perhaps you want them removed from your child's case.

During a lengthy hospitalization, one girl had various monitors attached by sticky patches. Because her skin was fragile, the doctor had decided to allow the patches to remain on until they fell off by themselves. One nurse (who the mother felt somewhat uncomfortable with already) came on shift and told the mother she was going to change the patches. When the mother suggested she check with the doctor before she did, the nurse agreed.

Then when the mom turned around for just a minute, the nurse ripped a patch off causing the child some discomfort and skin damage. The mother immediately made arrangements to talk with the nursing supervisor who removed that nurse from the case.

When the Person You Disagree with Is a Doctor. You can deal with that, too. If after discussing the problem with the doctor the two of you still do not agree, talk with the doctor who is in charge of that floor/ward or the medical service (specialty that the doctor practices) at the hospital. If you do not know who to approach, the hospital ombudsman or social worker can help you. In extreme cases, you may need to replace the doctor with someone who more closely meets your family's needs.

Another family had a daughter, Joanne, whose diagnosis is frequently fatal. During a hospitalization for flu symptoms, staff made a half-hearted attempt to put in an IV and, when that failed, told the mother that Joanne was receiving plenty of fluids by mouth. The problem was that she was getting sicker and her mom knew she was throwing up what appeared to be all the fluids she was taking in. The mom also knew she was dealing with residents and interns who were still somewhat inexperienced and Joanne's primary physician was depending on reports from those young doctors.

When the child's condition was obviously deteriorating, the mom decided to take things into her own hands. She was especially concerned that the staff attitude seemed to be that since her daughter was going to die anyway from her primary disability, nothing much should be done for her current illness.

The mom contacted the too-busy primary physician personally and told him that either Joanne got an IV and better care for her apparent symptoms of dehydration, or she wanted an ambulance to take her to another hospital where she would. Within the hour an IV was in place and her daughter was starting to feel better.

How Aggressive Should Treatment Be?

Joanne's situation brings up the whole concept of how aggressively you believe your child should be treated. Her mother believed that the flu was a temporary condition that did not need to result in her child's death and she was right. (As of this writing, several years later, Joanne is still doing fine.)

However, there may be times when you are faced with very gray areas in which to make life and death decisions. Please be sure that you have taken time to work out your intentions with your spouse or partner and you both agree on how you want these situations handled. If you are in serious disagreement, talk with your child's physician, a therapist, and/or your pastor, priest, rabbi, or other spiritual counselor. Develop a plan you can both live with so that if the worst happens, the disagreements over how to handle it will not tear apart your family.

Make absolutely sure your child's physician knows and is comfortable honoring your wishes on this subject. Allow for the fact that your choices may change over time. In addition, as your child grows up and gains a full understanding of his or her medical condition, you will need to consider (not necessarily grant) his wishes.

Most of all, remember that when you are dealing with hospitalizations, you are more than just your child's parent, you are the best advocate your child has. No one knows him better and no one cares more than you that he get the best care humanly possible.

Going Home from the Hospital

Once you have an anticipated date of release, you need to get busy doing the following so that everything will be ready on time for the trip home.

1. Talk with your child's doctor and other medical professionals who have been working with him in the hospital to determine what supplies you will need and what therapeutic activities you will be expected to perform.

While your child is still in the hospital and you can have professionals instruct you, practice any therapies, dressing changes, or other procedures that you will be expected to perform at home until you are comfortable with your ability to do them well. It is a good idea to get the medical professional to write down exactly what is expected of you (or take detailed notes yourself). There can be so much confusion involved in getting home and resettled that verbal instructions can be forgotten or misremembered.

2. Do you need any supplies you do not currently have on hand? Arrange to get prescriptions filled and equipment delivered a day in advance in case there are any hitches that have to be worked out. If you know you will need expensive new equipment, start immediately to research ways to get it paid for (See chapter 10).

3. Check with the billing office a day before you plan to leave to be sure all the paperwork is in order and will not delay your child's discharge.

4. Will you be dealing with any new professionals such as visiting nurses or therapists? Schedule their initial home visit before you leave the hospital. If they are not currently involved with your child they may want to visit in the hospital and consult with your child's physician before discharge.

5. Are there professionals you have dealt with before who need to be notified that you will be needing them soon? They could include respite workers, visiting teachers from the school district, or oxygen delivery people. Call them and arrange for the supplies and service to be in place when you need them.

6. Finally, be sure you or the hospital have arranged for transportation home. If you need an ambulance or other special vehicle you may need to order it at least a day in advance for nonemergency transport. Also, if your child has accumulated a tremendous amount of "stuff" in the hospital (such as plants, flowers, balloons, stuffed animals) start taking some of it home a day or two in advance. If there is a lot, consider offering some excess toys to the hospital for the playroom on the ward.

Take Care of Yourself So You Can Take Care of Your Child

Tired? If you've been staying with your child or shuttling back and forth between the hospital, your home, and your job, the idea of getting all these details taken care of can be daunting. You don't have to do it all yourself. There are people in your personal support network who can help. Maybe a friend can handle the calls to the school district. Your respite nurse can call the regular suppliers and get deliveries started again. The hospital social worker may be able to put you in touch with equipment suppliers you need now. Your spouse, parents, or siblings may be willing to make a few phone calls each or stand in line at the pharmacy to help you out.

If at all possible, plan to give yourself supportive help once you get home. If you have respite services, having the nurse come for a few hours a day as you get settled in at home can give you a chance to take a nap, go to the grocery store, or sit in the yard and decompress. If your child is still ill, consider having the respite nurse do a night shift or two so you can sleep for a night or more when you first get home.

No respite? Look to your network. If people ask what they can do, give them a specific chore such as, running to the pharmacy, dropping off a soup and salad for dinner (or even picking up fast food and delivering it), making some phone calls, or doing the laundry—whatever needs to be done.

Remember the Needs of the Rest of the Family

Your child and family will need your personal attention through the "re-entry" process and you need to catch your breath, too. Your child may be somewhat fussy for a while either because of discomfort or because he needs time to get over the stress of the hospitalization. Your spouse probably feels that he has been pulling double duty trying to keep the home fires burning and supporting you and your hospitalized child. A little extra attention can help ease any irritability he feels at the upheaval going on. Also, other children have undoubtedly had less of your time lately than they are accustomed to enjoying, so you will need to reassure them that life at home is returning to normal even though it may take some time.

Once Things Calm Down at Home, Remember the Hospital Staff

A final note about your experience with the hospital staff: it never hurts to be nice (you may have to go back there sometime). When you come home—especially from a long or stressful hospitaliza-tion—consider sending a thank-you note and maybe some candy. Perhaps you can bring a batch of home-made cookies to leave at the nurses' station when you and your child are back for a check-up.

If there were one or a few people who went far beyond the call of duty to help your child and you, write a nice thank-you note directly to each of those people and send a copy to their supervisor to put in their employment file. (This can help when they are up for a raise or promotion.) Everyone enjoys having their contributions recognized and a few minutes of your time spent writing letters now can result in an even better relationship with hospital staff people next time your child checks in.

13

When Home Is Away from Home

Making the Decision for Long-Term Residential Schooling

Some families reach a time when they realize that they need to consider a residential school for their child with a disability. This is certainly not an easy decision to come to or even think about. But, there can be family situations where placing your child in a residential school is the best and most loving decision for everyone concerned.

You may start thinking about the possibility of a residential school long before the need actually arises for a variety of reasons. Perhaps your child is becoming too heavy for you to handle (even with whatever equipment you have been able to acquire). Maybe your living arrangements are inaccessible (say, up three flights of stairs) and there are reasons why you cannot move. It could be that your child's medical problems have reached a level where reliable, around-the-clock care is necessary.

Your local schools may be hopelessly inaccessible and you fear the time and energy it takes to force them to change will take a heavy toll on your child. The school district may even bring up the possibility of helping you find a residential school (that the district will pay for) that will meet your child's physical and educational needs.

Other reasons that are not a direct result of your child's disability may come on slowly or drop full-blown into your lap. A serious illness of one (or the only) parent may make it impossible to care for the child at home. Sometimes economic necessity forces the caregiver to work full time and there is no reliable, competent replacement available.

There are times when the needs of other family members must take precedence. It may be time for parents who are completely physically and emotionally exhausted to take a year to regroup their own energies. Or, maybe, parents need to spend some time giving special attention to other children whose needs have been subordinated to the needs of the sibling with the disability too long.

There also may be times when a child who has a physical disability needs to go away for her own psychological good. One instance might be a child who has become socially isolated because of difficulties getting around at school and out of the home. This child could be terribly lonesome and welcome the opportunity to study, play, and live with others her own age. Another situation could be that the child has developed emotional problems as a result of her disability and needs a fresh start with people who are specially trained to deal with these problems.

Also, a family may decide that it wants a residential school for the child simply because it offers an opportunity to compete on a more equal field academically and participate fully in social and extracurricular activities designed to meet the special needs of students with physical disabilities.

The list could go on and on. The reasons why a family considers residential school are as varied as the individuals themselves.

When you are considering your options, you may be approached by family members or others who act as if you must not be much of a parent if you are willing to send your child away to school. They may tell you that if you just tried a little harder or did whatever it is they think you should do that you would not have to do this. They may even try to lay a real guilt trip on you. Don't let them do it.

When you make a decision out of love for your child, no one has the right to second guess you. You are not getting rid of your child; you are helping him build a better life right now and for the future. Besides, you will probably visit him regularly and bring him home for visits just as if you had enrolled him in an exclusive prep school.

In fact, you might find the comparison to a prep school a handy one to use so people realize you are not sending your son to some dank, medieval institution but to a private school that has wonderful programs, caring staff, and (probably) lovely grounds.

Evaluating Your Options

Decide on the kind of environment you want for your child. Do you want a school where there are students with a wide range of disabilities? For some students, that would mean that they fit in or will even be among the most accomplished if their only disability is physical. For other students, it is important to their self-esteem to be in a school where most of the students have disabilities similar to theirs. You are the best judge of the kind of environment that will be best for your child's personal development.

Go for the Best

What kind of education should you expect for your child who is in a residential school? The very best. Your child should be educated to the maximum level he is capable of accomplishing. That means that if your child is capable of doing academic class work good enough to graduate from high school, you should be sure the school you are considering is prepared to educate him and assist him in planning a post-high-school career whether it is in a vocational program or college.

Students who will not be able to meet the requirements for high school graduation might work toward a goal of a Certificate of Attendance or other recognition.

Choosing a School

Once you decide to explore the option of a private residential school, get information about several that appear to meet your child's individual needs. Your school district can help you learn of some schools you should consider. Another place to look is *Exceptional Parent* magazine, which often has information about different schools. One outstanding resource is the National Association of

Private Schools for Exceptional Children (NAPSEC) which offers a free listing of member schools that might be suitable for your child. To access this service, call the NAPSEC office at (202) 408-3338. (It is in Washington, D.C., if you want to allow for time zone changes between you and them.) They will ask you five simple questions before they compile a list of schools individually selected for your child. The questions are:

1. What is your child's age?
2. What is your child's gender?
3. What kind of a facility are you looking for (i.e., day, residential, or summer program)?
4. In what state or region of the country would you like the school to be located? This service can be especially helpful if you are contemplating a move to another part of the country and are not familiar with the schools there.
5. What is your child's disability?

Once you have the names of several schools, call or write to them and ask for information about the school and its programs. When you have read the material and narrowed the choices down, try to visit each school you are seriously considering. When possible, bring your child along.

When you (and your child) visit a school, try to do the following to get a complete picture of what life at this school offers:

Allow plenty of time to walk around campus. Meet with personnel. (Try to be sure you meet with the people who would be teaching and caring for your child, not just the marketing people for the school.) What is the staff to student ratio? Ask if your child can join in a few activities while you're visiting.

Eat a meal with the students if possible. Would your child enjoy the food and the ambience?

Visit with the people who provide special educational services. If you want your child to receive special educational services such as psychological counseling; physical, occupational, and/or speech therapy; adaptive physical education and recreation; nursing services; and social work, make sure you visit with the professionals who provide those services.

Look at the bedrooms. Will your child have a good balance of privacy and social interaction? Will your child be able to express his personality in the way his room is decorated?

Will any necessary medical supervision be handled in a way you are comfortable with? Will the school personnel encourage your child's growth and independence by allowing him to continue to perform any medical tasks he currently does (like give himself shots)? Will they teach him new medical self-help skills as he matures? More important, will they follow your directives in the event of a medical emergency?

Request names and phone numbers of parents of current students you can call for references. Then do it. While the school will undoubtedly give you the names of parents they know are satisfied, these parents are also likely to share personal stories about their child's attendance at the school. This may help you get a more complete picture of what your child may experience there.

Smoothing the Transition

Once you have chosen the school, it is time to begin the transition process. Debra Flanders at Crotched Mt. School in New Hampshire says that the most important thing for parents to do is make sure their child does not feel abandoned at the school.

The key is to let your child get settled in, but keep in touch. Flanders says that at Crotched Mt., parents often stay at a guest house on campus for the first few days and use that time to help their child get settled in and instruct school personnel about their child's personal preferences. She then suggests that the parents leave, but when possible, come for a visit in a week or two so the child will realize that his parents will keep returning for him.

While Crotched Mt., like many residential schools, has a year-round program, it also has regular "vacations" during the year and encourages families to bring their students home at those times.

How to Ease Your Child's Adjustment

Some things you can do to help your child make the adjustment include sending a photo album from home, audio and/or video tapes of home activities (like singing favorite songs, reading favorite stories) that can be played during moments of homesickness, frequent phone calls to and from home, and letters and cards. Be sure your child takes favorite "lovies" such as stuffed animals or other items that will be familiar in the new environment.

Your child will probably miss you, but maybe not as much as you miss him. He will be very busy in a new environment doing new things, making new friends, and having fun in a setting that is especially designed to make life easier for him. There will also be staff who are completely focused on helping him—a near impossibility for you when you are taking care of him, your home, family, job, and all your other responsibilities, without having fresh staff to relieve *you* three times a day. Some parents have found that a day or two after they brought their children home from residential schools for a visit, their kids were eager to be back at school where there was more going on and where their friends were.

When Should Your Child Come Home for Good?

There are any number of reasons why your child will spend only a short time (anywhere from months to a few years) in a residential school. Perhaps there was a family situation that has been resolved. Maybe the home school district has implemented changes that were necessary for your child to attend locally. Sometimes a child who has a physical disability develops emotional problems in adolescence and the family realizes that she needs more help than they are able to offer. A year or more in a residential school with other children who are dealing with the same problem may give her the support and insight she needs to get on top of her problems.

Some times families who have enrolled a child in a residential school decide to end the enrollment. If you have reason to believe your child is unsafe, you should absolutely do what ever is necessary to change the placement. However, that is extremely unlikely to happen. If the school decides that the placement is not working, there are legal steps they must take before they request that you find another school for your child.

What is more likely is that you do not think that your child is making the progress you anticipated at this particular school. When this is the case, before you withdraw your child, you should reexamine the reasons you choose a residential school. Ask yourself what the expectations of your child's doctors and therapists were before your child enrolled in the school. Are there reasons why those expectations have not been met (or maybe they have been met but you were hoping for more)?

Whenever you have questions, you should bring them to the school administration and expect thorough answers. In any case, you should expect to have a review of your child's progress at the school at least once year.

The residential school option has proven to be a very positive experience for many children. If you decide that this is the best choice for your child, take all the time you need to find the right school, give your child as much help as you can in making the transition, visit regularly, and stay in close touch with your child and the school.

Group Homes and Foster Care

There are other out-of-home options you may need to consider for your child at some time. Depending on your family's situation, you may choose to look into group-home placement or foster care.

Group Homes

Group homes often have an ambience similar to living at any home. Either resident adults or a hired staff care for the personal needs of the residents. You are most likely to find these locally through referrals and may even need to help organize and/or raise funds to support this option. Your social worker can help you find any group homes in your area, tell you about their requirements, and help you access any programs that can help cover the costs.

Foster Care

This option is usually available through your county's welfare department when it becomes impossible for you to care for your child at home. It will probably only be available until your child reaches the age of majority in your state. One real benefit is that having your child in foster care can give you a window in time to get your life organized and prepare to have your child come home permanently. On the other hand, if you are not working toward bringing your child home, you may feel some pressure to make your child available for adoption by others.

Sometimes the hardest part of loving a child is letting him go on to the situation that is best for his personal growth. And when attending a residential school, moving to a group home, or going to foster care is the right answer for your child, you can be proud of the sacrifice you are making now to help your child build a better future.

PART III

Details of Daily Living

14

Personal Hygiene

In the normal course of things, you take care of all the hygiene needs for your infant. Then, as the child grows, he begins to take care of some simple needs like hand washing and eventually takes care of all his personal needs.

But if your child has a physical disability, you may find that normal progression altered, if not eliminated entirely. Yet, your child still has the same physical and emotional needs as his peers when it comes to handling his personal hygiene. By remembering that, you can ease the transitions when your child is able to take on some personal care tasks for himself and work with him to find acceptable methods of coping when he is unable to handle tasks where he (understandably) wants more privacy.

Bathing

One area that comes up early is bathing. Even when your child is very young, you may find yourself projecting into the future and worrying about issues of personal privacy. This can be a special concern for families with a physically disabled daughter who needs to be lifted in and out of the tub as well as washed.

If the father is the strongest and best one to do the lifting—and the daughter is dealing with issues of puberty—there can be some concern about sexual issues. It is important that you as parents take time to recognize and work out a plan to deal with this situation.

One very wise young woman in her late teens was asked how she felt about the fact that her father was the one who bathed her. Was this a problem for her? Did it make her uncomfortable? Her answer was a refreshing surprise to the listeners who had been anticipating a difficult emotional situation. She simply said, "He's not a man, he's my father."

Be aware that, for whatever reason, the answer may not be as simple for your family. If you need help sorting out the needs of various family members, talk with a physician or therapist you trust and work out a plan you are *all* comfortable living with. At the same time, remember, it may simply be a nonissue for some families.

Toileting

Another area that tends to bring out a lot of emotional discomfort is toileting. When your child is an infant, it probably never occurred to either of you that there could be a problem. But, once a child is at an age where toilet training should have been completed (whether that was possible or not), you will need to be sensitive to your child's needs. If your son or daughter notices that other family members use the bathroom with the door closed or do not undress in front of others, make every effort to allow them the same privacy.

Once in preschool or school, children are toileted by aides. Take a few minutes to show the aides any personal preferences your child has. Remember that the aides usually want to help, but may not deal well with feeling that their competence is being challenged. It helps to couch it in terms like, "I know you are very experienced at this, but I'd like to show you how Sally likes to be toileted so we can work together to help her."

Also, from time to time, talk to your child about how toileting is going at school or with babysitters. And, as your child gets older, talk about good and bad "touching" and why you should be told if "bad touching" happens. If you are not sure how to handle this topic, your local library may have books on the subject or be able to refer you to local organizations that can give you pointers.

By elementary school, your child will want privacy. If the handi-capped toilet is in the same room that all the other girls (or boys) use, it may be a good idea to work with her aide (or even through her IEP, see chapter 8) to find a time when the bathroom is not being used by others so your child and the aide can have privacy.

Depending on your child's needs, it could be important for the toilets at home or at school to have attached seats with back and/or arm supports. Seat belts are a good idea for children who have the potential to have muscle spasms or weaknesses that can cause loss of balance. It is also a good idea to have a foot support so feet do not dangle, especially if your child has abdominal muscle weakness. Supporting the feet and legs gives a better sense of balance and makes it easier for your child to have a bowel movement. A short child may need a step-stool to get up on the toilet seat comfortably.

Some children may need to use catheters for urinating and adopt a regular program of bowel care. If this is a fact of life for your child, work with your medical professionals to teach your child to handle as much of the process as he or she is physically and emotionally able to deal with. You may be able to build your child's skills over time to where he or she is able to handle toileting needs alone. Any degree of control that your child can achieve over the process will strengthen his or her self-image and independence.

Menstruation

Parents of daughters face an additional challenge at puberty (which one mother devoutly hoped would be preceded by the Rapture— sometimes called the end of the world). When a girl first menstruates, it is a time filled with emotions, hormones, and questions. And it's not much easier for parents.

How your family handles this will depend largely on how you have handled the personal hygiene situations up to then. It may be a very natural inclination to have only female family members help with toileting during the monthly period. However, that can really ham-string any woman who takes on that responsibility.

If her father has been handling her personal needs all her life, the daughter is likely to accept his help in toileting and changing pads during her period. Actually, under these conditions, the person having the hardest adjustment is likely to be the father.

To make life easier for everyone, treat your daughter's periods as a natural, normal occurrence (and maybe with a little humor if it fits your family's style). That way, no one person will be held hostage to your daughter's monthly cycle. Remember the young woman who, when asked about being bathed by her father, said matter of factly that he wasn't a man, he was her father. A loving father will often be willing to learn how to help his daughter during this time, and a loving mother will support the father's learning curve.

While it may seem easier to handle everything yourself, it is important to recognize that the more people your daughter is able to direct to help her with her personal needs, the stronger her independence skills will become.

15

Skin Care and Protection

Great stuff, skin. It gives you something warm and soft to hold onto when you hug your child. More important, the skin is our largest organ and works constantly to protect all internal systems. Yet, when someone has a disability, his or her skin can become unusually vulnerable to damage from a variety of sources.

Bathing

Cleanliness is every bit as important (if not more so) for a child with a disability as it is for any other child. For children who need a great deal of assistance, regular bathing can be difficult. When it is impossible to do a tub bath or shower every day, you can still bring a basin of warm water, a washcloth, and some soap to your child's bed and do a quick scrub and rinse. When you do this, pay special attention to the armpits and crotch where perspiration or body fluids can cause irritation. Then dry the skin carefully.

When your child's skin gets dried thoroughly once or more a day it tends to heal faster. If irritation from moisture does cause itching or mild rashes, you might consider lightly powdering the area after it is dry. Your pharmacist can explain the benefits or drawbacks of different powders, some of which are medicated. If you do use powder, be sure to put it only on the affected area and do not apply it in a way that causes a big cloud of powder to arise. If your child inhales the powder it may cause respiratory problems. If the rash or itching is still not relieved, call your child's doctor for assistance in clearing up the condition before it becomes a more difficult problem to deal with.

Preventing and/or Treating Pressure Sores

Keep an eye out for pressure sores that may be forming. A pressure sore is the skin's way of telling you that it is being worked too hard and getting too little blood flow through it.

Common causes include pressure from braces or sitting or lying in the same position for long periods of time. Even an incorrectly fitted shoe can put undue pressure on an ankle. A child who leans on an elbow too much may find that rather than getting tough and callused, the skin develops pressure sores.

In the early stages, a pressure sore looks like a red spot that can be warm to the touch and turn white when you press on it. If the spot does not return to the same color as the rest of the skin within about 10 minutes of relieving the pressure, it is time to take action.

Do whatever you can do to relieve the pressure on the site. If it is caused by a brace or body jacket, it is time to visit the orthotist to have the item adjusted or replaced.

If the pressure sore is on the back, lower back, or hips, and your child spends a great deal of time sitting down or in a wheelchair every day, it is time to look into acquiring a new cushion. The company that supplied your child's wheelchair can advise you on the different types of cushions that are available. They may even have samples that you can see and try out.

During warm weather, sitting still for long periods of time on cushions covered with materials that do not "breathe" can accelerate skin breakdown. When that happens, consider putting a layer of sheepskin (fluffy side up) on the seat so your child is sitting directly on it. That will help air circulate and keep clothes and skin drier.

Real sheepskin is expensive, but there is a synthetic sheepskin fabric that you can always get through medical supply houses that works very well and it can be machine washed and dried (low setting). You may be able to find the synthetic sheepskin at an affordable price through a large fabric store.

In a pinch, you can fold a bath towel and put it over the cushion. If the towel is damp when you remove your child from the chair, replace it with a fresh, dry towel.

Other spots to keep an eye on include the areas that take a lot of weight when lying down: hips, shoulders, and knees (also pay attention to her ears if she lies on the side of her head). When pressure marks are a result of her sleeping position, consider getting a larger piece of sheepskin for your child to sleep on. "Egg carton" foam pads placed over the mattress also help skin heal during sleep. Change your child's sleeping position more frequently during the night if skin problems are developing.

Pressure sores on the elbows are especially difficult to deal with, especially if your child uses elbows for balance when sitting at a table or even to hold her head up when tired. You might start by offering a cushion of some sort for under her elbow (even a layer or two of sheepskin sewn together with a rubber sheet—use one of those flat rubber jar opening pads—glued to the back so the cushion will not slip on the table). You can even sew elbow pads into favorite shirts or sweaters to give a little extra cushioning. A slender child could use absorbent tennis wrist bands pulled up to the elbow to cushion skin and keep it dry.

When Pressure Sores Become Dangerous

If you do not catch pressure sores in the early stages, they will get worse. The affected skin will become dark red or bluish-red and is probably cold to the touch. That is because the circulation is extremely poor here and the skin is literally dying. It is not just the top layer of skin either. The damage can go through all the tissue right down to the bone.

When the skin breakdown becomes advanced, open sores often occur. These can present a real danger of allowing infection to enter your child's body at a point where it is already damaged. Open sores require very special care and sometimes even surgery. They take a long, long time to heal and are nothing to mess around with. When the skin is dramatically disolored and does not return to normal color within 15 to 30 minutes of having the pressure removed, contact your child's physician or physical therapist for expert help.

Maintaining Good Blood Circulation

Along with good nutrition, good blood circulation is the key to having healthy skin. Good nutrition is discussed in chapter 16, and like good nutrition, good blood circulation is an area where you can make a positive difference.

There are two ways you can really help enhance your child's blood circulation. One is through physical therapy; the other is through massage.

Physical Therapy

One type of physical therapy you may do with your child every day is range-of-motion exercise. This technique moves the body in normal patterns (like flexing a knee). Doing this exercises whatever muscle tissue your child has, encourages blood circulation, and helps delay or prevent joint contractures (tightening) that can occur when joints are inactive. Your child's physical therapist can teach you simple stretching and range-of-motion exercises that will benefit your child. You may find that after a session, your child feels invigorated in much the same way that you do after an exercise session.

Whenever possible, it is important that the exercises be done daily, which means they can become pretty boring. Fight it. The health benefits are too important to let them slide. To keep things interesting, play favorite music in the background or put an exercise video on the VCR and work out your own variations on the in-structions they give. (Let's face it, "kick right, kick left" is just the same if you are lifting your child's leg or lifting your own.) If you can handle the noise level, an adolescent may be more motivated to cooperate if you do the exercises along with MTV after school.

Massage Therapy

Another option to enhance circulation and skin condition is massage therapy. There are many different kinds of massage—some more forceful (and more or less desirable) than others. Your medical professionals can refer you to massage therapists whose techniques may be helpful to your child. If your physician does not currently work with massage therapists, you might contact a physiatrist (a doctor who specializes in physical medicine and rehabilitation), health organization, or area hospital or medical school for referrals.

The field of massage therapy is gaining respect as practitioners prove the value of their work. Unfortunately, there are still some people who claim to be practicing massage whose focus is not on medical benefit. So do not start looking for a masseuse in the Yellow Pages. Go with referrals from medical professionals you trust.

Protecting Skin Against the Elements

Use common sense when you are dealing with your child's skin care needs. A bad sunburn can make anyone feel uncomfortable, but if the sunburn is on skin that is bound by braces the next day, your child will be severely uncomfortable. Be sure that when your child is exposed to enough sunlight to give him a tan or burn that he is wearing a good sunblock.

In cold weather, frostbite can be a real problem. Your child's good skin condition will be more successfully maintained if you keep it dry and within normal temperature ranges and covered to protect it from freezing weather.

Every family has questions that are unique to them. The questions may concern pretty normal things. In that case, you may want to go back to your parents, other family members, and friends for advice. If the situation you are dealing with is related to your child's disability, you may find that talking with other parents facing similar problems provides you with useful advice. Health organizations and medical professionals may also be excellent sources since they are likely to have worked with many families facing the same problems you face today. It is likely that someone has already invented the wheel you are looking for, but it may take some searching on your part to find the answer that already exists. Be patient and tenacious and you will find the answers you seek.

16

Handling Medications and Food Restrictions

Nearly every child requires some medications from time to time, but a child with a disability is more likely to take medications some or all of the time. Your child may get prescriptions for medications from his doctors and/or you may purchase some nonprescription medications at the drug store yourself. (These are called over-the-counter or OTC.)

Medicines Prescribed by Your Doctor

Since your child is likely to have more than one doctor, you may find that several people are prescribing medications. It is critical that each physician is aware of every medication your child is taking (whether it is prescribed or OTC) to be sure different doctors are not prescribing medicines that work against each other or have dangerous side effects when taken together.

When a doctor prescribes a new medication, be sure you understand what it is and what it is expected to do for your child. Ask:

- What are the benefits of this drug?
- What are the potential side effects?
- What is the dosage?
- What is the timing of the doses? Does three times a day mean at each meal or exactly eight hours apart?

- What should you do if a dose is missed? Skip it entirely or make it up right away? Don't guess.
- Should the medication be taken with food or on an empty stomach?
- How will the drug interact with any prescribed or OTC medications your child is already taking? Don't count on your doctor to remember every other medication your child is taking. He or she should ask, but it is your job to keep him up to date—and bring up the subject if he forgets.

Choosing a Pharmacist

You *must* also be sure to choose a competent pharmacist who keeps meticulous records. That way the pharmacist will hopefully spot any incompatible medicine combinations before your child takes them. Your pharmacist should be someone you can talk to comfortably and ask about any concerns you have about the drugs that have been prescribed.

Taking Medications Safely

If the medication is a liquid and the instructions call for a specific measured dose (like one teaspoon), do not assume that your household teaspoon is exactly the right size. Your pharmacist can provide you with accurate spoons or oral syringes that will measure the liquid precisely.

Inform your child's doctor(s) and pharmacist of any over-the-counter medicines your child may be taking—even aspirin or cough syrup. That way they can alert you to any potential problems from mixing medications.

When the prescription (like an antibiotic) is only for a short term, it is very tempting to stop giving it when your child starts to feel better. However, the infection that brought on the need for the medication may not be fully defeated even though your child seems better. It is just as important to get the right dose at the right time on the last day of the course of treatment as it is on the first.

Keep the poison control phone number in your community

posted at your phone. Children are curious and will often eat things that can be harmful. Youngsters have been known to gnaw on house plants, nibble on medications they find in Grandma's purse, sip cleaning supplies, or accidentally ingest too much of a prescribed medication. If your child does manage to swallow the wrong things, call that number immediately. They will tell you what to do.

When Your Child Refuses to Take Medications

Even the most motivated child can get to a point where he is tired of the pills, injections, inhalation therapies, and other medicines. You might be, too, but you understand the importance of maintaining the treatment program even when your child is going through a phase where he decides to make it as difficult as possible in hopes that you will give up.

Several years ago a boy who needed daily shots reached that point. A procedure that normally took a few minutes became an hour-long struggle and his mother says that the whole family was becoming "a bunch of basket cases" as they tried to deal with his attitude. Her pediatrician came up with a plan that relieved the situation in only a few days. He told her that instead of trying to do the shot at home, she should pack her son up and take him to the pediatrician's office. There, instead of the warm welcome he was accustomed to, the boy was whisked to a treatment room, given his shot (that his mother had prepared and brought with her), and told curtly that they would see him tomorrow. No stickers, no fancy bandage, no friendly pat, no fun. He didn't like that much.

By the third day, he had decided to take his act to the office. He was fighting the staff so actively that they had to hold him down to give him his shot. It hurt.

On the way home, he told his mother than she gave better shots and he wanted her to start giving them again. To everyone's relief, he has stuck by his decision to cooperate and the shots have not been a serious problem since.

If *your* child becomes very uncooperative in taking medications, talk to your physician about the situation. He or she may have equally creative ways to help your child get past this stage.

In addition, talk with your child about how he perceives the situation. Does he understand the reason for and importance of the medication? Is there something about the way the medication is administered or the timing that he wants to change that the doctor (and you) will agree to?

Sometimes it can be a surprisingly little thing. Linda developed an intense dislike for applesauce. It turned out that for years her mother had sometimes hidden her medicine in it and she had decided that applesauce was not good stuff to eat. She told her mom and since Linda was older now, she was able to start taking her medicine in pill form. Linda was then more agreeable to taking her medications—but she still won't eat applesauce!

The Food Connection

Do you whip out the orange juice at the first sign of a cold? Does flu season mean that you keep chicken soup handy? Then you already understand how the foods your child eats can have an effect on the body similar to that of a medication.

Unfortunately, some foods can also have a negative effect on your child's health. At times, you will notice the culprit yourself. Some foods seem to increase mucous production in the throat and lungs causing coughing and congestion. Other foods may trigger asthma attacks. Sometimes your child's doctor will point out that certain foods are likely to have effects that can range from mild nuisance to life-threatening depending on your child's disability.

Even relatively young children can learn that eating certain foods is bad for them. But you need to stay on top of the situation. Especially if your child's food sensitivity is serious, you should be sure that any teachers, caregivers, or parents/caregivers of playmates also understand how important it is to avoid certain foods. Otherwise, well-meaning adults may push dangerous "treats" on your child, thinking they are doing the right thing.

There are wonderful, tasty substitutes you can offer your child in place of forbidden substances. For instance, there are now several types of dairy-free frozen desserts for people who cannot ingest milk. However, your child will need to be very aware of which foods are OK and which ones are not. In this case, one variety of the nondairy frozen dessert looks and tastes very much like regular ice cream. A child who does not clearly understand the difference might accept ice cream at a friend's home without realizing the difference. You may find it best to go without the substitute foods until you are absolutely sure your child is old enough to understand the difference and monitor his own eating.

Good Nutrition Is Crucial

It is always a good idea to talk with your child's doctors about any food restrictions that are prescribed or any you are thinking about instituting yourself because you need to be sure that any diet plan supplies well-balanced nutrition.

Your doctor may be wonderfully competent as a physician, but lack a strong background in nutrition. If so, you may want to ask for a referral to a professional nutritionist or dietitian. When possible, it is best to work with someone who is familiar with your child's disability and any special dietary requirements resulting from that medical condition.

If your physician does not work with a nutritionist, you may be able to find one through a diagnosis-specific organization. For instance, a family dealing with cystic fibrosis might contact their local Cystic Fibrosis Foundation for referral to a nutritionist or dietitian who can help them find special predigested baby formulas and supplemental vitamins as well as develop high-calorie, high-protein diets for older children.

It is not uncommon for children with disabilities to develop weight problems. Inactivity can lead to overweight and some conditions can lead to excessive thinness. When the scale tips too much in either direction, it can add medical complications to your child's condition. A good dietitian can help you work out ways to enable your child to reach a healthy weight.

In addition to working on menus, your dietitian will be able to educate you about the nutritional value of different foods, "shake"-type food replacements for children who find chewing tiring, and ways to choose or prepare foods to meet special chewing or swallowing needs.

17

Choosing Attractive, Functional Clothing

The clothes we all (regardless of your age) wear influence how others relate to us and how we feel about ourselves. It goes without saying that your child's clothes need to be age appropriate, comfortable, functional, and attractive (although you and your child may disagree on what constitutes attractive clothing).

Never underestimate the importance of dressing your child in age-appropriate clothing. If your child is very young, that means shopping for coveralls or sweet dresses. As much as possible, dress your son or daughter like their peers, even if that means letting them wear items decorated with media-hyped cartoon characters they adore. Children who are able to assist in dressing themselves often prefer items with Velcro fastening strips to zippers or small buttons. If a clothing item has buttons, you may be able to resew buttons to the front of the garment and sew Velcro strips to the back of the button site.

As your child grows, keeping the clothing age appropriate becomes more difficult. One problem is that it is easier to simply buy necessary clothes and bring them home than it is to take a child shopping. The good news is that more and more stores are building accessible changing rooms. The bad news is that they rarely have a padded bench in the room to place your child on while you change garments.

Going Clothes Shopping

If your child's disability is such that you need to be able to have him lie down on a surface so you can change the clothes, you have several options. Ask if there is a "mothers'" room with a changing table (if your child is still very small) or a bed you can use. Ask if there is an employees' lounge or nurse's office that has a bed or couch. In a pinch, some families have used the tops of large, sturdy boxes in store rooms. The last resort (unless you have more time than you know what to do with) is to take your child shopping, pick out all the clothes she likes, buy them all, take them home to try on, and return whatever you decide not to keep. (If you need to buy underwear or swimsuits, ask about the store's policy on returning these items before you try this.)

Tailoring Clothes to Fit

Some disabling conditions can result in your child being shorter or much thinner or heavier than peers and you may find that it is very hard to find clothes that fit in the same styles that others the same age are wearing. Sometimes you can do simple alterations to take clothes in or shorten hems. If you do not sew and do not have friends or family who can help, you can often find a good seamstress through your dry cleaner.

One option you might want to consider is making some clothes. You can look at the pattern books with your child and pick out styles that are fashionable as well as functional. Then you can choose fabrics in the currently popular colors, prints, and fibers. When you make the garments yourself (or with help from your seamstress), you can build in allowances for bulky braces, add some length to the back of the seat for a child who uses a wheelchair and is tired of pants that pull down in the back, put in Velcro or elastic waists for easy dressing, and make sure garments sit or drape nicely for the way your child lives.

Be sure that the garments are similar to what peers are wearing. Children really want to look like their friends and many will feel that wearing "different" clothes sets them apart even more than their disability does. Sometimes parents pick what is easy for them, such as sweat suits. Sweats are great, but if everyone else is wearing jeans to school, they can look out of place. Unfortunately, it is very difficult to find jeans that have an elastic waist in sizes for older kids.

Shoes Complete the Outfit

Another note here about looking different. Even if your child is not walking, shoes are an important clothing item. At the very least, they protect feet from accidental bumps and keep them warm in cold weather. Most important is the fact that *everyone* wears shoes.

All styles will not work in all cases, but if your child wears shoes, sneakers, or sandals every day, his heel cords are less likely to tighten to where he cannot wear shoes any more. If the heel cords do tighten, you can do exercises you learn from a physical therapist to loosen them, have him wear short leg or ankle braces until the cords lengthen and stabilize, or have a shoemaker alter the shoe by cutting out part of the back of the heel.

If your child does walk but needs special orthopedic shoes, making them look more acceptable may sometimes be a problem. Ask the professional who fits and/or builds your child's shoes for suggestions on how to make them look more like the shoes other kids are wearing. Beyond that, on a minimum level, you may be able to get fancy shoe laces to dress them up with a splash of color. On a maximum level, you might consider going to a good shoe repair shop and having them dyed your child's favorite color.

Foul Weather Clothes

Foul weather gear can sometimes create a lot of stress between you and your child. You want your child to stay warm and dry, but she wants to look like everyone else. If you insist on getting your way, you are likely to find that more and more often, the coat or rain gear comes home in the backpack or somehow "gets lost." Work with your child to find rain and snow clothes that work and are functional and you will find that they are likely to be worn—not lost.

If a raincoat is too difficult to get on, check out lightweight windbreakers that are made out of water-resistant fabrics. If those are still too difficult to manage, consider a hooded poncho made from waterproof material. An umbrella can be handy, but only if your child is strong enough to hold onto it and can control it while moving around outside.

In terms of warmth, a heavy coat is not always the best answer, especially if the weight and bulk of the sleeves makes it difficult to drive a wheelchair or use other devices. The best way to keep warm is to wear layers of clothing to trap body warmth. When your child finds it difficult to get into a coat or to get around once he is in it, there are other ways to handle the situation.

For days that are cool, start with an undershirt. Then add a tee shirt, blouse/shirt, or sweatshirt. If it is really cool, consider an undershirt, blouse/shirt, and sweatshirt or sweater (sleeveless is best for a child with weak arms). Those three layers will provide a surprising amount of protection from the cold and may still be comfortable in a warm classroom. In really cold weather, you may find that several layers over your child's trunk and a good, lightweight windbreaker (and gloves or mittens) will provide enough protection.

Underwear

Comfortable underwear is an important element to any wardrobe. Undershirts provide warmth in cool weather and protection from skin damage from body jackets and braces on the torso. Underpants and undershirts should be made of a fabric that will wick moisture away from tender skin.

For boys, the choice between boxers and briefs will depend on several factors including whether he can pull them up himself and whether he can move around to eliminate wrinkles that can irritate skin. If one style of underwear is more functional than another and dad happens to wear the other, consider asking dad to get a few in your son's style and wear them. It helps dad understand (and hopefully share with his son) the benefits and shortcomings of the chosen style. It also helps your son see the choice as a positive masculine style instead of something different because of his disability.

For girls, cotton underwear is the most practical and comfortable. Today, companies make cotton underwear in a variety of colors or patterns and some even have ruffles to make them prettier.

A note for parents of children going through toilet training. "Big kid" panties can be presented as a very desirable item. Whether your child is a girl or boy, you might consider allowing one pair of "big kid" panties per day. If they stay dry, the child can keep them on all day. If there is an accident, there should be no anger, recriminations, or shaming from you. Just clean the child up and go back to diapers for the rest of the day. If your child is physically ready and motivated, you will be surprised at how quickly toilet training is completed when he or she controls the reward.

Accessories Make the Outfit

Just looking at the kids streaming out of your neighborhood school will convince you that they believe that accessories are just as important as adults do. They just choose different accessories.

When your child tells you how much he wants a particular accessory, pay attention. He is trying to show how he defines his place in his social group. You may be able to help with some things fairly easily. A child with cerebral palsy who has a problem with drooling may object strongly to wearing a bib to school even though you know it is a practical way to protect other clothing. But if you think for a minute, a colorful bandana tied around the neck with most of the fabric in front serves the same purpose without the "babyish" connotations of wearing a bib. Bandanas are also inexpensive (so you can buy lots of them) and are easy to wash.

Other popular accessories with a fashion angle can include backpacks, sneakers, and hair ornaments. Hats, tee shirts, and jackets displaying team logos are often popular as are items featuring entertainment figures from movies, television, or cartoons. Remember that your child wants to fit in with her peers, and when possible, provide her with the accessories that she wants because "everyone" has them. It is much more important to say "no" to what everyone else is doing when it comes to inappropriate behaviors than it is to say no to fashion accessories.

Catalog Shopping

A marvelous catalog called Avenues Unlimited sells clothing specifically designed for people who use wheelchairs. Their clothes often include special tailoring to make them easier to put on and fit better in a sitting position. They have specialty items like gloves designed for people who push their own wheelchairs and wheelchair accessories such as cup holders and backpacks. There are also cushions for wheelchairs or beds and hard-to-find items like snow chains for wheelchairs, inflatable bathtubs, and shampoo basins that can be used in bed. In addition, they offer tailoring on the clothes they sell to make them fit better and be more functional.

Their clothes are primarily designed for adults, although teens can wear many items and some, like rain ponchos, come in youth sizes. They stock casual clothes like jeans as well as dressier items. They plan to offer a catalog targeting children in the future; it may be available when you read this. To get a current catalog, call (800)848-2837.

18

Responsibilities You Must Fulfill

Long-Range Planning

Does the idea of long-range planning seem somewhat absurd considering how much you already have to do every day? In truth, everything you do has an element of long-range planning already built into it. Every time you choose to do a therapy with your child, every time you help your child reach an educational goal, you are working toward the goal of a better future.

The key to long-range planning is to set a goal (or set of goals) and then set intermediate goals to help you get there. For instance, perhaps your ultimate long-range goal is for your child to live a happy, productive, independent adult life.

Right now that goal may seem unattainable as you are tied up in an apparently endless round of medical appointments, therapy appointments, and meetings with school personnel and social workers, and the list goes on and on.

You are also very aware of the problems your child has and any negative assumptions people may have made about your child's future. But in the long run, it doesn't matter what other people think. It is what you and your child think that will have the greatest impact on the future.

Let me tell you my family's story. My daughter, Abby, was born with spinal muscular atrophy (a progressive paralysis) and initially was not expected to live long enough to start school. While many children with her diagnosis do die young, many others live to adulthood and lead productive lives. My husband and I chose to raise Abby as if we expected her to grow up, which meant setting goals for her.

Some goals we set were educational. She was expected to do well in school. She started in a preschool program for children who have orthopedic disabilities and was fully mainstreamed starting in kindergarten. The major reason we had her mainstreamed was so that she would grow up accustomed to living in the real world since she did not need a sheltered setting. We also felt she would have more challenging academic programs in regular schools. To her credit, she accepted our educational goals as her own and became a good student throughout her school years.

Some goals we set were psychological. We wanted her to be able to deal with her peers and adults comfortably and competently. To achieve this, she joined Scouts, a sports league, and Sunday School.

Abby also did public appearances for the Muscular Dystrophy Association from the time she was a preschool student. She loved those appearances at first because there always seemed to be a deli tray and she went straight for the salami. As time went on, Abby became quite a ham and enjoyed the appearances for the attention. Then as she grew, she started looking at the people working different professions at these events and considering them as career options.

As often happens, the contacts she made doing volunteer work opened other doors for her. Abby did a little modeling, some industrial movies, and got to know more about careers in the entertainment industry.

Now she is a college student living 400 miles away from home in an apartment on campus with her live-in aide. She is medically classified as quadriplegic and can do relatively few things for herself, but she is living a full and exciting life and studying with an eye to becoming a professional in the public relations field (or a screenwriter, if that works out).

Would Abby be there if we had not set goals for her and taught her to set goals for herself? Not likely. If we had bought into the medical advice that she would probably not live long and focused our energies on making life easy right then, she would probably still be alive, but she would be sitting at our home or in a nursing home watching television all day instead of planning to possibly write for it.

The goals we set for our daughter may be somewhat different from the goals you set for your son or daughter. As your child grows, you may also need to revise your goals and fine tune them as your child's own talents and preferences emerge.

If you have already started setting goals for your child and your family, good for you. If not, the box below shows a simple format you can use to help you get started. Try it out as an exercise first. Then, if your child is old enough to participate, work with him or her to formulate the actual goals you will work with. Your child is much more likely to cooperate and work eagerly toward goals that he has had a hand in setting.

Goal Setting Exercise

- List the goals you have for your child.
- Prioritize them. Start with #1 for your most important goal(s) down to #5.
- Pick a #1-level goal to use for the rest of this exercise.
- Write down the date by which you plan to accomplish this goal.
- List the steps that have to be taken before that goal can be realized.
- Put those steps in the order in which they must occur or in which you want them to occur.
- Give each step a deadline.
- Plan to recognize and celebrate each step as you and your child accomplish it. When possible, have the recognition relate to the accomplishment. For instance, if the goal is for your son to learn how to dress himself and the step is learning to tie his shoes, then maybe the recognition might be a new pair of sneakers he has been wanting.
- Realize that you have to work toward each step of each goal in a regular way. Post the goals and steps where you and your child can see them every day. Check them at least once a week to be sure you are continuing to work toward your ultimate goals. If the steps can be broken down to daily or weekly increments, consider making a chart

(Continued)

(Continued)

and using some gold stars or cute stickers to post on it every time he successfully completes an activity leading toward the goal.

- Allow for the human factor. Time frames may have to be adjusted from time to time to reflect interruptions in life. An illness, vacation, or other event can mean that your short-term goals need to be put on hold for a little while. When you are ready to get back to them, set a new deadline that is realistic and doable.

- Do not underestimate the importance of placing a deadline on your goals. As a wise person once said, a goal is a dream with a time limit on it.

- Use this same process to set goals for yourself. Don't make the mistake of letting your whole world revolve around your child for the next 18 years. You would be doing yourself, your disabled child, and your whole family a great disservice.

Look to Your Future

With a little luck (and a lot of work), your child will grow up and lead an independent adult life. What will you do with yourself then?

This is not to say that you should run out today and get a job or become the queen of volunteers in your town. But you are likely to have better emotional health and deal better with your child's independence if you have a life of your own. There are few sadder sights than parents clinging to their caregiver role to their grown children because they have nothing else going on in their life.

Actually, you will find yourself gaining and polishing many new skills over the years as you raise your child and advocate for him in different settings. Perhaps you will decide to pursue new options in the future based on what you are learning now.

Many families find that it works best for them if one parent is a full-time caregiver when they have a child with a serious disability. If that is you, remember that there are a lot of other ways to have a part of life that is just for you without getting a paycheck. Consider taking a class one evening a week. Have a movie night or bowling night with good friends. Join a club. Teach something you already know. Take up a new hobby, especially one that gets you out of the house from time to time. Volunteering at your child's school and/or diagnosis-related organization is also good, but keeps you oriented toward your child's needs. It can be really nice to have someplace or some organization you go to where you are yourself first and your status or work as a parent is completely separate.

Also, remember that your child is always watching you. If he sees you act as if you believe there is more to life than a disabling condition, he will believe that, too. If he sees you keeping at least some active involvement in the world as an independent adult, he will see a role model for what he can look forward to when he grows up.

Why You Must Make Out a Will

Even now, when you are so busy taking care of the tremendous volume of details it takes to care for your child with a disability, your whole family, and everything else, there is one more detail you absolutely must attend to: making out your will. It may seem that your lifestyle is mostly crisis management—and since the will can wait a while longer it will have to—but it really needs to be a priority. If you and your spouse were to die, what would become of your child(ren)? How would your assets be distributed?

These questions are especially important to you as the parent of a child with a physical disability. Depending on what state you are living in at the time of your death, your son or daughter is not considered an adult until they are either 18 or 21 years of age. A child younger than that will be assigned a guardian by the courts if you have not provided for one in your will. Even if you have an informal, verbal agreement with a family member, that agreement (as the old joke goes) is not worth the paper it isn't written on.

Emotions can ride high during a family crisis and other relatives who you did not think would be best to raise your child may petition for guardianship and win. If you are leaving your child considerable assets and insurance money, the chance to control those assets may also influence some family members to try to gain guardianship.

Another important point is that if you are counting on personal friends or godparents to step in and raise your child, put it in writing. If you have any family, the courts are not likely to allow nonrelated persons to be your child's guardian unless you have specified your wishes in a will. If you do choose to name a nonrelative as guardian, be sure to specify why (again, in your will) so that the court will have your reasoning if a relative attempts to overturn your will and become the guardian.

In some cases, you may even wish to nominate a person who you would prefer to have as a guardian for your child even if he or she is a legal adult. If you believe your child may not be able to make competent decisions and control his own life, or if he has over-whelming difficulties in communicating his wishes, you may want to nominate someone you would like to have as a guardian in your will. Then, if you die, your adult child can either benefit from the guardian-ship or petition the court to set it aside.

As your child grows, you should also consider letting him know where you keep your will and basically what it says. For instance, a teenager should know (and possibly participate in choosing) the guardian you have selected. He should also have some idea of what will happen to any assets you have if you should die. You don't need to obsess on it, but he should know if there will be enough money to see him through college and why you have put it in trust or handled it some other way.

The other major reason to make a will is to be sure that your assets are distributed and used the way you want. There are two major factors to consider: how much each heir gets and how they get it.

If you do not have a will and your spouse is deceased or you are unmarried, your state laws decide who gets how much. If you have more than one child, the state will probably divide the inheritance equally among them regardless of their individual levels of need.

When you make out a will, you can specify any distribution you want. Have you already provided for the college education of your other children and you want to assure that your disabled child will always be able to afford any medical care she needs? You can arrange for her to inherit the bulk of your estate. Is it a family tradition that everyone works to get the oldest through college and he helps the next and so on? Then you may want to direct your funds very differ-ently.

What form do you want the inheritance to take? This question is critical if your child is likely to have access to government benefits at some time in his or her life. The way the laws are written in the United

States right now, your child may have to spend all or nearly all of his assets before qualifying for government programs that can assist him with basic living expenses and medical care. Even if your child does not qualify now, she might qualify after your death (if your lawyer writes your will correctly).

Trusts

The best way to give your child the benefit of his inheritance while still protecting his access to government programs is to leave his inheritance in the form of a trust. Your trust will designate a trustee who can be one of your relatives, a friend, your attorney, your banker, or other responsible person who will manage the assets of the trust and pay them out to your child in the time frame and under the conditions you have specified.

The trustee does not have to be the same person you name as guardian of your child(ren). That way, if you decide that your child is most likely to thrive in the custody of your sister, but she can't balance a checkbook, your child can have the loving home he needs and have his financial future protected, too. You might choose another adult as trustee or specify a bank to act as trustee.

A trust will generally pay out sums of money to support your child and pay educational and medical expenses. When there is a chance that your child will qualify for government assistance, you will want to look into two specific kinds of trusts: a "Special Needs Trust" and "Discretionary Trust."

The assets placed in these trusts can only be used for certain limited purposes, but will allow your child the benefits of the trust while still qualifying for government programs. You can also give the trustee discretion to terminate your trust at some point in the future if the laws about qualifying for government benefits change, or medical advances cure your child's disability, or other unforeseen events occur.

The trust will normally continue until your child reaches the age that you have specified for the proceeds to be turned over to her (unless it is one of the types mentioned above). Many people set an age of 25 or 30 even for nondisabled children to inherit so they will (hopefully) have reached a level of maturity where they can handle the money responsibly. You might consider making your child a co-trustee when she is two or three years from inheriting so she can spend time working with the trustee and learning how to manage the assets.

On the other hand, you can set up the trust so your child benefits from it, but does not ever actually receive all the assets. You can specify that your child will benefit from the trust for his or her lifetime and then the remainder can be given to other children or grandchildren, charity, or whomever you have chosen.

Choosing a Guardian

Naming a guardian for your children in your will may very well be the single most important step you can take to ensure that if you die your children will be raised the way you would have wanted.

While the natural assumption is that your child will live with the person you name as his guardian, that is not necessarily true. The guardian will make decisons about your child's living arrangements, but that could be in her home, a group home, a residential school or college, or even an institution.

As your child grows up, he may need to move from one setting to another, perhaps from the guardian's home to a college dorm. Another child may need a residential school and then move on to a group home. Whatever your child's changing needs are, his guardian will be responsible for making decisions about his living arrangements until he reaches adulthood.

When considering the choice of a guardian, ask yourself the following questions:

1. *Who is most likely to give your child emotional and psychological support?* It should be someone who already likes your child and knows something about his disability and the demands it puts on the family. This person should be able to advocate for your child with medical, educational, and social service entities. When all other factors are equal it can help if the guardian you nominate can enable your child to keep attending the same school and seeing the same medical professionals so there is some continuity in his life.

2. *Who is physically able to handle the challenge?* Your parents may be wonderful people (they raised you, didn't they?), but are they strong and healthy enough to take care of your child's physical needs now and the needs you foresee in the future? At age 70, will your parents be up to helping your then strapping 16-year-old in and out of bed and wheelchair? Will they have the stamina to take care of all his personal needs and still be able to have a life of their own?

3. *Does the guardian you are considering share your values?* This is especially important if your children are still very young. It is one thing for someone to say they will raise your child with religious or social values very different from their own, but it is incredibly difficult to do it over a lifetime. With older children, you have had more time to teach them the values you cherish and living a few years with someone who has somewhat different values is less likely to be a long-term problem, but is still something to think about.

Religion can be a special concern since faith, or a lack thereof, can determine both a person's attitudes and activities. Children get a great deal of their social identity from the rituals they are a part of. If you are Roman Catholic, you may be looking forward to your child's First Communion. If you are Jewish, a Bar or Bat Mitzvah. Will the person you nominate as guardian see to it that your child fully experiences these spiritual milestones?

4. *Does the person share your feelings about the extent and quality of the medical care you want your child to receive?* The guardian may have to make decisions about everything from quality of life, to kinds of acceptable risks, to life or death decisions for your child. Whether you believe doctors should treat your child's problems very aggressively, let nature take its course, or somewhere in between, you will want to choose a guardian who feels as you do. A medical emergency is no time to expect someone else to put aside their personal philosophy to try to decide what you would have wanted and then advocate your position effectively with the doctors.

5. *Does the potential guardian have the financial resources and/ or talent for dealing with bureaucracies?* This is important to be sure your child is taken care of if your assets are not enough to pay everything it costs to raise him.

6. *Does your child like this person?* This is not necessarily required under law, but it sure helps. As your child grows, you should stay aware of which people your child enjoys spending time with and who shares her passions. (A child with a flare for the arts could be seriously bored in a family where order and regulation are most highly prized as personality traits.)

7. *Does the potential guardian's lifestyle mesh with your child's needs?* The person who has the best personality match and whose values are closest to yours may be almost a gypsy whose job leads to frequent moves or whose idea of a great weekend is mountain climbing (not an option with your son's wheelchair). Is the potential guardian willing to make the sacrifices in his personal life that would be necessary to care for your child or are you willing to consider that the guardian may need to place your child in a residential facility to guarantee the necessary level of care?

8. *Have you asked him or her?* Just because you nominate someone, it does not in any way compel him or her to take the job. You should have gotten their permission to name them and spent some time telling them what you would hope they would do and what resources will be available to them. If you are naming a married person, don't automatically think you have to name the spouse, too. Divorce happens. If your married sister becomes your son's guardian and then divorces, who should get custody if your will named both her and her husband as joint guardians?

9. *Have you considered naming an alternate guardian in case the person you nominate cannot or will not perform?* Life never stands still. The person who agreed to be nominated as your child's guardian may since have changed his mind, moved to an area where your child could not get the quality medical care she needs, become ill or disabled himself, or just changed his lifestyle to the extent that caring for your child is no longer feasible. That person (especially if he is much older than you) may not live or stay healthy long enough to finish the job, especially if your child is still very young. Also, something could happen during the years the person is acting as guardian that would cause him to step aside. At that time, the court would give serious consideration to the alternate you had named in your will.

One Last Thought

Sometimes there are worse things than dying. People become disabled and are not able to handle their personal and financial responsibilities either temporarily or permanently. You should have a Durable Power of Attorney that states your wishes and names the person who can make medical, financial, and all other decisions for you if you are not able to make them for yourself.

When you are ready to make a will, set up trusts, and sign a Durable Power of Attorney, find a professional lawyer who specializes in helping families like yours. Remember, law is like medicine; even after working at it for years, professionals still say they are "practicing." Unless you are a lawyer, it can be dangerous to assume that you know more as an amateur than someone who has been working at it for a long time. There are kits you can buy or generic forms you can fill out, but if you make even a small mistake your will could be invalidated or your wishes could be misunderstood.

If you do not know a good lawyer, one place to call is the local charity or social service agency you already deal with. They may know lawyers who specialize in making sure the needs of children with disabilities are protected.

Do not feel shy about asking the lawyer what his or her fee schedule is. At this writing, a simple will for you and your spouse will probably run a few hundred dollars. If you need a complex will because of your personal situation, the fees may be more. If you cannot afford the full fee right now, talk to the lawyer about whether she will allow you to make monthly payments until the bill has been paid in full.

In the event your family has been seriously financially stressed by taking care of your disabled child, check with Legal Aid to see if any lawyers are willing to do discounted or pro bono (free) wills for families in your situation.

What ever you do, don't put this off. With any luck, your will will gather dust for years to come. You will raise your children and grow old watching them flower into very special adults. However, if your luck runs out, you can be sure theirs doesn't. Your will is a lasting gift of security that only you can give them.

PART IV

Appendixes

Appendix 1

Specialists You Should Know

Many different medical specialists may contribute to your child's care at different times. Some, like the pediatrician, will be a constant. Others, such as neurologists, pulmonologists, or endocrinologists, may be consulted from time to time.

Following is a listing of many types of medical specialists—some psysicians, some not—you may deal with. Many of these specialists may use the term "pediatric" in their title to show they specialize in dealing with children needing this medical speciality.

acupressurist. Uses thumbs, fingers, palms, or elbows to apply specified pressure at specified points on the body to relieve pain, tension, or stress.

acupuncturist. Administers specific therapeutic treatment for symptoms and disorders by inserting needles of various lengths at locations known to be efficacious to those disorders.

allergist/immunologist. A physician who diagnoses and treats diseases and conditions caused by allergies or immune problems.

anesthesiologist. A physician who administers anesthetics to render a patient insensible to pain during surgery and other medical procedures.

audiologist. A professional trained to evaluate and help with a suspected hearing problem.

cardiologist. A physician who is specially trained to diagnose and treat heart problems.

chiropractor. A medical professional who diagnoses and treats musculosketal conditions of the spinal column and extremities to prevent disease and correct physical abnormalities believed to be caused by interference with the nervous system. Chiropractors are not physicians. (See also OSTEOPATHIC PHYSICIAN.)

dentist. A medical professional who diagnoses and treats diseases, injuries, and malformations of teeth, gums, and related oral structures.

dermatologist. A physician who diagnoses and treats skin conditions and diseases.

dietitian. Teaches patients and families nutrition and how to plan meals, especially for people with special dietary needs.

DO. See OSTEOPATHIC PHYSICIAN.

ear, nose, and throat specialist. See OTOLARYNGOLOGIST.

family practitioner. A physician who provides comprehensive medical services for the whole family.

general practitioner. A physician who provides comprehensive medical services for patients of all ages. Often used as a primary physician.

geneticist. A specialist in the study of the branch of biology that deals with heredity.

immunologist. See ALLERGIST/IMMUNOLOGIST.

internist. A physician who diagnoses and treats diseases and injuries of internal organ systems.

masseuse. A person trained in massage which may be useful to help increase circulation, relieve soreness, and relax muscles.

nephrologist. A physician who diagnoses and treats conditions affecting kidneys.

neurologist. A physician who diagnoses and treats organic diseases and disorders of the nervous system.

occupational therapist. A trained medical professional who deals with activities of daily living (eating, dressing, grooming, etc.) by evaluating current function level and working with the patient to develop new skills.

oncologist. A physician who diagnoses and treats cancer.

ophthalmologist. A physician who is specially trained to diagnose and treat (including surgery) eye problems.

optometrist. A professional trained to perform eye examinations and dispense eye glasses—not a medical doctor.

oral surgeon. A dentist who performs surgery on the mouth, jaws, and related head and neck structures.

orthodontist. A dentist who examines, diagnoses, and treats abnormalities in the development of jaws, positioning of teeth, etc.

orthopedist. A physician who specializes in diagnosing, preventing, and correcting skeletal deformities.

orthotist. A professional who constructs braces, splints, and other devices under the direction of a physician.

osteopathic physician. A medical doctor who is also trained to use manipulative therapy when needed. Osteopathic physicians (DOs) are found in every medical speciality and their licensing and training are the same as those of allopathic physicians CM, D.S. in the U.S., and Canada.

In the U.K. they are not licensed medical doctors, but provide the same services as chiropractors do in the U.S.

otolaryngologist/otorhinolaryngologist. A physician who specializes in problems of the ear, nose, and throat.

pediatrician. A physician who plans and manages the medical care program (dealing with both preventative and urgent care) for a child from birth through adolescence. This doctor is often the child's primary physician.

pharmacist. A professional who dispenses prescribed medications and answers questions about medications including side effects and potential problems with drug interactions.

physiatrist. A physician who specializes in physical medicine and rehabilitation.

physical therapist. A trained professional who evaluates function and deformity and plans and executes exercise and training to maintain the best possible function and prevent or slow down deformities.

podiatrist. A medical professional who diagnoses, treats, and performs surgery on diseases and deformities below the ankle.

psychiatrist. A physician who focuses primarily on the biological aspects of mental illness. Psychiatrists tend to rely on medication as an important form of treatment. In addition, they must be licensed and can also be board certified.

psychologist. Counsels families or individuals dealing with emotional problems. Also may give psychological tests for diagnostic purposes. All 50 states require that psychologists be licensed although requirements for licensure requirements vary by state and most require a doctoral degree (Ph.D., Psy.D., or Ed.D.) as a minimum.

radiologist. A physician who diagnoses and treats diseases using X ray and radioactive substances. May also examine internal structures and functions of the organ systems.

respiratory therapist. A trained medical professional who provides care to enhance respiratory status including chest physical therapy, bronchial drainage, and oxygen. Works under the supervision of a physician and by prescription.

social worker. A professional who helps facilitate communication among the family, health care professionals, and community and governmental programs that may be useful.

speech therapist. A professional who diagnoses and develops treatment programs for patients who have speech problems.

surgeon. A physician who performs surgery to correct deformities, repair injuries, and improve function in patients.

urologist. A physician who diagnoses and treats (often surgically) abnormalities of the genital/urinary systems.

Appendix 2

Organizations That Can Help

There is a tremendous variety of organizations you can contact for information, support, and services. Of necessity, this chapter lists groups that are active nationally and internationally. These groups can refer you to local chapters where they exist. They may also be able to give you referrals to other organizations that will be useful to you.

You may find small groups in your community that you will want to get in touch with. These groups can be especially helpful when you need the support of talking to another family and tips on finding the best doctors and hospitals for children who have disabilities like your child's. In addition, local groups can often offer assistance in dealing with school districts and other bureaucracies that may not be as helpful as you need them to be.

You can find local groups in a variety of ways in addition to referrals from national organizations. First, start with your physician or the social worker at your hospital. Then you can check with your librarian (many of them keep special listings of area organizations). If you still cannot find what you want, try contacting the school district and ask to talk with the head of special education and/or physical and occupational therapy programs if it has them.

Still stumped?

Check the government listings in the phone book for titles of departments that sound like they assist disabled children. Finally, many newspapers have columns where you can write a letter asking for information (often without having your name published). Then the columnist will either give you the answer you are seeking or ask other readers for input.

Back to librarians for a moment. Your librarian may have access to computerized databases that will be useful to you. Some may be listings of organizations or individuals who can help. Other databases record straight information. For instance, on MEDLINE you can run a search of published material on your child's disability by using only a few key words. Several databases are listed later in this chapter.

If your child's disability is an uncommon one and you want to get in touch with other families, many of the organizations listed here can put you in touch with others dealing with the same problem. Remember, they will need to protect your confidentiality and that of the other family, so they may need to take your message and get back to you.

Another outlet for you is to write to *Exceptional Parent* magazine and ask them to publish your letter in their "Parents Search" column. If your letter is chosen to be published, other families dealing with the same problem are likely to get in touch with you through the magazine. Many families have found support this way, although it takes a while for the letters to get published. Write to Parents Search, *Exceptional Parent* Magazine, 209 Harvard St., Suite 303, Brookline, MA 02146-5005.

So here is the listing. Don't be shy about calling a group even if you're not sure it is exactly what you need since it is likely to be a good referral source. Also, when you call, it is often helpful to ask for the patient services department or public information department since they are most likely to be the persons you want to speak to directly.

You will note that there are often toll-free phone numbers as well as regular phone numbers. Be aware that the toll-free numbers will usually not work across national boarders (for example, from the United States to Canada or vice versa) and you will have to use the regular number in these cases.

The listing includes a brief description of the mission, services, and/or goals of each organization. This does not by any means fully describe what the organization has to offer, but it might help you sort through things. For instance, many families are not aware that the Muscular Dystrophy Association deals with 40 neuromuscular diseases, the Arthritis Foundation works with 100 different diagnoses, and the Epilepsy Foundation of America assists with more than 20 seizure disorders.

The federal government offers a wide range of clearinghouses and information centers, each focusing on specific areas of concern. When you call them, you can ask them to send you publications that provide referrals and answer your questions. Since they tend to offer pretty much the same services, they are listed here with only a phone number to get in touch with them, but no further description of their mission.

If you cannot find your child's diagnosis (or you do not have a specific diagnosis yet), start with the organization that comes closest to dealing with your child's medical condition and go from there.

Organizations Offering Assistance

Amputation

NATIONAL AMPUTATION FOUNDATION
73 Church St.
Malverne, NY 11565
(516)887-3600

The National Amputation Foundation is comprised of amputee volunteers who offer their support to fellow amputees and their families because they believe a real need exists to provide the patient and family with the opportunity to relate to another person who has been through a similar experience. They also offer literature and a newsletter.

Arthritis

AMERICAN JUVENILE ARTHRITIS ORGANIZATION

A Council of the Arthritis Foundation comprised of children, parents, teachers, and others concerned specifically about juvenile arthritis. See ARTHRITIS FOUNDATION.

ARTHRITIS FOUNDATION
1314 Spring St., N.W.
Atlanta, GA 30309
(800)283-7800
(404)872-7100

The Arthritis Foundation is the only national, voluntary health organization that works for all people affected by any of the more than 100 forms of arthritis or related diseases. Volunteers in chapters nationwide help to support research, professional and community education programs, services for people with arthritis, advocacy, and fund-raising activities.

NATIONAL ARTHRITIS AND MUSCULOSKELETAL AND SKIN DISEASES
INFORMATION CLEARINGHOUSE
(301)495-4484

Asthma and Allergy

ASTHMA AND ALLERGY FOUNDATION OF AMERICA
1125 Fifteenth St., N.W., Suite 502
Washington, D.C. 20005
(800)7-ASTHMA
(202)466-7643

Through its nationwide network of chapters and support groups, the Asthma and Allergy Foundation of America provides educational and emotional support to its clients. AAFA also funds research for improved treatments and, ultimately, a cure.

NATIONAL INSTITUTE OF ALLERGY AND INFECTIOUS DISEASES
(301)496-5717

Ataxia

NATIONAL ATAXIA FOUNDATION
750 Twelve Oaks Center
15500 Wayzata Blvd.
Wayzata, MN 55391
(612)473-7666

The National Ataxia Foundation attempts to locate people and families with hereditary ataxia in order to provide them with information and direct them to resources knowledgeable about their problems. The Foundation deals with all types of hereditary ataxias (such as Friedreich ataxia) and closely related conditions such as peroneal muscular atrophy (Charcot-Marie-Tooth disease), hereditary spastic paraplegia, ataxia telangiectasia, and others. Also see MUSCULAR DYSTROPHY.

Brain Injuries

BRITISH INSTITUTE FOR BRAIN INJURED CHILDREN (BIBIC)
Knowle Hall
Bridgwater
Somerset TA7 8PJ
England
Phone: 0278 684 060

BIBIC is a registered charity whose function is to teach the parents of brain-injured children individually designed programs of stimulation therapy.

Cancer

CANDLELIGHTERS CHILDHOOD CANCER FOUNDATION
c/o American Cancer Society
7910 Woodmont Ave., Suite 460
Bethesda, MD 20814
(800)366-2223

The Candlelighters Childhood Cancer Foundation works to educate, support, serve, and advocate for families of children with cancer, survivors of childhood cancer, and the professionals who care for them. It also offers separate newsletters for parents and for children who currently have or have survived cancer.

CORPORATE ANGEL NETWORK, INC. (CAN)
Westchester County Airport, Building One
White Plains, NY 10604
(914)328-1313

CAN is a volunteer organization that matches empty seats on corporate aircraft flying on business trips with cancer patients (children can also bring both parents if space permits) traveling to and from treatment. The service is free and financial need is *not* a requirement. There are some requirements of the patients, including that they be traveling between home and NCI-recognized centers for treatment, consultation, or check-up; be able to walk onto the aircraft unassisted; and do not require life support systems or special services. CAN cannot guarantee space at any given time, but has already flown over 6,000 patients through the cooperation and generosity of more than 550 participating corporations.

NATIONAL CANCER INSTITUTE
(800)4-CANCER

Cerebral Palsy

UNITED CEREBRAL PALSY ASSOCIATIONS, INC.
1522 K Street N.W., Suite 1112
Washington, D.C. 20005
(800)USA-5UCP
(202)842-1266

The mission of UCP, Inc., is to have a positive impact on the quality of life for persons with cerebral palsy and others with severe disabilities and multiple service needs (and their families) as well as to prevent cerebral palsy and minimize its effects.

Cleft Palate

CLEFT PALATE FOUNDATION
1218 Grandview Ave.
Pittsburgh, PA 15211
(800)24-CLEFT
(412)481-1376

Founded as a public service of the American Cleft Palate-Craniofacial Association which has membership in 40 countries, the Cleft Palate Foundation's primary purpose is to educate and assist the public regarding cleft lip and palate and other craniofacial anomalies and to encourage research in the field.

Craniofacial

AboutFace INTERNATIONAL
99 Crowns Lane, 3rd Floor
Toronto, ON
Canada M5R 3P4
(800)225-3223
(416)944-3223

Through its offices in Toronto, Canada (where AboutFace began in 1985) and the U.S. (since 1991), AboutFace functions as a support and information network concerned with facial difference. AboutFace offers support through networking families who share similar concerns and chapter activities. AboutFace promotes public awareness and education through publications, an annual family conference, etc. In addition, the group offers a database of member's insurance experiences and volunteer insurance advocates in many geographical areas who provide advice and information.

AboutFace U.S.A.
P.O. Box 737
Warrington, PA 18976
(800)225-3223
(215)491-0603

See AboutFace INTERNATIONAL.

THE NATIONAL ASSOCIATION FOR THE CRANIOFACIALLY HANDICAPPED (FACES)
P.O. Box 11082
Chattanooga, TN 37401
(800)332-2373

FACES has a threefold mission: (1) financial assistance for transportation, food, and lodging to enable clients and one companion to travel to specialized craniofacial medical centers for treatment; (2) public awareness and understanding of craniofacial anomalies and the children who have them; and (3) information and support to craniofacially handicapped persons about specific conditions and resources available to them.

Cystic Fibrosis

CYSTIC FIBROSIS FOUNDATION
6931 Arlington Rd.
Bethesda, MD 20814-5200
(800)FIGHT-CF
(301)951-4422

The Cystic Fibrosis Foundation is dedicated to funding research to find a cure for cystic fibrosis and improving the quality of life for people with cystic fibrosis through research, medical care, public policy, and education.

Deaf/Hearing Impaired

DB-LINK
The National Information Clearinghouse on Children Who Are Deaf-Blind
345 N. Monmouth Ave.
Monmouth, OR 97361
(800)438-9376 (Voice)
(503)838-8776 (Voice)
(800)854-7013 (TTY)
(800)503-8821 (TTY)

DB-LINK is a federally funded information and referral service that identifies, coordinates, and disseminates information related to children and youth who are deaf-blind (ages 0 to 21 years). The organization responds to questions from families and educators on a wide range of topics including education rights and services, medical and social services, technology, employment, and independent living. DB-LINK can also provide referrals to other organizations such as state departments of education, research projects, local and regional organizations and advocacy groups, parent groups, and medical centers.

NATIONAL INSTITUTE ON DEAFNESS AND OTHER COMMUNICATION DISORDERS INFORMATION CLEARINGHOUSE
(800)241-1044 (voice)
(800)241-1055 (TT)

ROYAL NATIONAL INSTITUTE FOR DEAF PEOPLE
105 Gower St.
London
WCIE 6AH (England)
FAX:071 388 2346

The Institute offers a wide range of services for persons who are deaf or hard of hearing. The services include interpreting, Typetalk, assistive devices, and comprehensive services.

TRIPOD
2901 N. Keystone St.
Burbank, CA 91504
(800)352-8888 (National Voice/TDD)
(800)2-TRIPOD (California Voice/TDD)

Serving children who are deaf or hard of hearing, Tripod offers family support based on a total communication philosophy which supports a child's strengths and fosters clear communication in school and at home. Tripod offers a toll-free hotline called the Grapevine which provides families with the support they need to make confident, well-informed decisions.

VOICE FOR HEARING IMPAIRED CHILDREN
124 Eglinton Ave. West, Ste. 420
Toronto, ON M4R 2G8
Canada
(416)487-7719 (Voice and TDD)

VOICE offers support and practical assistance to hearing impaired children and their parents. It supports early testing and identification of hearing impairment, early and appropriate use of hearing aids, advocacy with governments and school boards, and early and intensive auditory verbal therapy.

Dental

NATIONAL FOUNDATION OF DENTISTRY FOR THE HANDICAPPED
An affiliate of the American Dental Association
1800 Glenarm Place, Suite 500
Denver, CO 80202
(303)298-9650

The NFDH organizes and operates programs in many (but not all) states, providing essential dental care for persons of all ages who are physically, medically, or mentally disabled. People are treated in existing dental offices and clinics and there is normally no charge to the patient family.

Diabetes

NATIONAL DIABETES INFORMATION CLEARINGHOUSE
(301)468-2162

THE AMERICAN DIABETES ASSOCIATION
1660 Duke St.
Alexandria, VA 22314
(800)232-3472
(703)549-1500

The American Diabetes Association works to prevent and cure diabetes and improve the lives of all people affected by this condition through education and services to people with diabetes, their families, health care professionals, and the public.

JUVENILE DIABETES FOUNDATION INTERNATIONAL
432 Park Ave. South
New York, NY 10016
(800)JDF-CURE

The Juvenile Diabetes Foundation International was founded in 1970 by parents of children who have diabetes who were convinced that, through research, diabetes could be cured. The Foundation has chapters from coast to coast and around the world that work to support research efforts.

Disabilities (General)

CONTACT-A-FAMILY
16 Strutton Ground
London SWIP 2HP
England
Helpline Phone: 071 222 2695

Contact-A-Family is a national organization in England that provides information and support to parents whose children have disabilities. It has a network of support groups that offer information about rare conditions. In addition, it has helpful publications and telephone support through the Helpline.

DIAL UK (Disablement Information and Advice Line)
Park Lodge
St. Catherine's Hospital
Tickhill Rd.
Balby
Doncaster
S. Yorks DN4 8QN
England
Phone: 0302 310123

DIAL UK is the headquarters of a network of 100 centers that people with disabilities can call for advice on all aspects of disability. The centers are all run and staffed by persons who have personal experience with disabling conditions.

DISABILITY SCOTLAND
Princes House
5 Shandwick Place
Edinburgh EH2 4RG
Scotland
Phone: 031 229 8632

Disability Scotland is the national organization that provides a resource for all people with disabilities in Scotland.

MARCH OF DIMES BIRTH DEFECT FOUNDATION
1275 Mamaroneck Ave.
White Plains, NY 10605
(914)428-7100

While the March of Dimes Birth Defect Foundation focuses primarily on prenatal topics, they also serve as a clearinghouse for families searching for information about their child's birth defect, especially families dealing with rare conditions. It can link families to support groups or other families in similar conditions; some chapters help these support groups get started. With a vast network of volunteers from the health care field, the Foundation can often link families to other sources of assistance such as medical and social services. Check your phone book for a local chapter, or call the number above.

NATIONAL EASTER SEAL SOCIETY
230 West Monroe St., Suite 1800
Chicago, IL 60606
(800)221-6827
(312)726-6200 (Voice)
(312)726-4258 (TDD)

The National Easter Seal Society provides quality rehabilitation services, technological assistance, information on disability prevention, advocacy, and public education programs. The organization works with people of all ages who have neurological/neuromuscular, communication, orthopedic, social/psychological, learning and/or developmental, and other disabilities. Easter Seals also assists families with disability screening and preventive programs.

EASTER SEAL SOCIETY (Canada)
Suite 200, 250 Ferrand Dr.
Don Mills, ON M3C 3P2
Canada
(800)668-6252 (Canada only)
(416)421-8377

Through its regional offices, the Easter Seal Society provides direct services, programs, research, advocacy, and public education to help children with physical disabilities achieve their full individual potential.

NATIONAL INFORMATION CENTER FOR CHILDREN AND YOUTH WITH DISABILITIES (NICHCY)
P.O. Box 1492
Washington, D.C. 20013
(800)695-0285 (Voice/TT)

NICHCY is an information clearinghouse that provides free information on disabilities and disability-related issues. It is operated by the Academy for Educational Development and focuses on children and youth (birth to age 22).

NATIONAL INFORMATION CLEARINGHOUSE FOR INFANTS WITH DIS-ABILITIES AND LIFE-THREATENING CONDITIONS
(800)922-9234 (ext. 201)

A joint project of:
Association for the Care of Children's Health
7910 Woodmont Ave.
Bethesda, MD 20814
(301)654-6549
    and
Center for Developmental Disabilities
University of South Carolina
Columbia, SC 29208
(803)777-4435

The National Information Clearinghouse for Infants with Disabilities and Life-Threatening Conditions is a national information and referral system created to support infants who have disabilities and their families by providing information about services available in their community or nationwide. For assistance, call the toll-free telephone number.

Dysautonomia

DYSAUTONOMIA FOUNDATION, INC.
20 East 46 St., Room 302
New York, NY 10017
(212)949-6644
(212)263-7225
With chapters in the U.S., Canada, Great Britain, and Israel, the Foundation supports medical research and clinical care for children with familial dysautonomia. At their evaluation center at New York University Medical Center, it also offers comprehensive care through periodic evaluations, personalized treatment plans, and access to the most current information on the condition.

Dystonia

DYSTONIA MEDICAL RESEARCH FOUNDATION
One East Wacker Dr., Suite 2900
Chicago, IL 60601-2001
(312)755-0198
The goals of the Foundation are to advance research into the causes of and treatments for dystonia; to build awareness of dystonia in the medical and lay communities; and to sponsor patient and family support groups and programs. It offers many publications including the excellent *Guidebook for Families: Special Education Rights.*

Epilepsy

EPILEPSY FOUNDATION OF AMERICA
4351 Garden City Dr.
Landover, MD 20785
(800)EFA-1000
(301)459-3700
The Epilepsy Foundation of America's goals are the prevention and cure of the more than 20 different seizure disorders, the alleviation of their effects, and the promotion of independence and optimal quality of life for people who have these disorders.

Eye/Vision

AMERICAN COUNCIL OF THE BLIND
Washington, D.C.
(800)424-8666
(202)467-5081

A national organization of State Councils of the Blind, see CALIFORNIA
COUNCIL OF THE BLIND.

CALIFORNIA COUNCIL OF THE BLIND
3919 W. Magnolia Blvd.
Burbank, CA 91505
(800)221-6359 (CA only)
(818)557-6372

Affiliated with the American Council of the Blind, the California Council
offers scholarships to deserving blind students based on need and/or academic achievement. They also offer other services which are more targeted
toward adults such as low-interest loans to enable blind people to purchase
equipment they need for employment (like talking calculators, etc.).

DB-LINK
The National Information Clearinghouse on Children who are Deaf-Blind
345 N. Monmouth Ave.
Monmouth, OR 97361
(800)438-9376 (Voice)
(503)838-8776 (Voice)
(800)854-7013 (TTY)
(800)503-8821 (TTY)

For the complete explanation, see listing under "DEAF."

ROYAL NATIONAL INSTITUTE FOR THE BLIND
224 Great Portland Street
London WIN 6AA
England
Phone: 071 388 1266

The Institute works to alleviate the problems caused by vision problems by
providing information and over 60 services to persons who are blind or who
have lost much of their sight.

Growth Disorders

BILLY BARTY FOUNDATION
929 W. Olive Ave., Suite C
Burbank, CA 91506
(818)953-5410

The Billy Barty Foundation assists people of small stature with medical
referrals, employment opportunities, adaptive aides, and information on
many topics of interest to Little People. The Foundation also offers schol-

arships to Little People attending schools all over the U.S. and has special funds at the Growth Clinic at Cedars-Sinai in Los Angeles and the International Center for Skeletal Dysplasia at St. Joseph's Hospital in Towson, MD, to assist families attending those clinics with transportation and lodging costs. BBF is the only agency staffed by and for Little People.

HUMAN GROWTH FOUNDATION
7777 Leesburg Pike
Falls Church, VA 22043
(800)451-6434
(703)883-1773

The Human Growth Foundation helps individuals with growth-related disorders, their families, and health care professionals through education, research, and advocacy. It publishes a monthly newsletter, serves as an information clearinghouse, and works through local chapters.

LITTLE PEOPLE OF AMERICA
(800)243-9273 (Information line)

While Little People of America is primarily made up of adults who have severe short stature, average-sized parents may join the Parents Auxiliary.

SHORT STATURE FOUNDATION
17200 Jamboree Rd., Suite J
Irvine, CA 92714
(800)24-DWARF
(714)474-4554

The purpose of the Short Stature Foundation is to provide service, information, and advocacy to enhance the positive well-being and independence of short-statured/dwarfed individuals. Through their helpline, (800) 24-DWARF, they offer dwarf group contacts, products and services, and referrals to medical practitioners and personal counselors closest to the caller's locale.

Heart

AMERICAN HEART ASSOCIATION
7272 Greenville Ave.
Dallas, TX 75231-4596
(800)242-8721
(214)706-1341

The American Heart Association supports professional and public education, community service programs, and research devoted to reducing disability and death from cardiovascular diseases.

NATIONAL HEART, LUNG, AND BLOOD INSTITUTE
(301)251-1222

Hemophilia

CANADIAN HEMOPHILIA SOCIETY
1450 City Councillors St., Suite 840
Montreal, Quebec, H3A 2E6
Canada
(514)848-0503

The Canadian Hemophilia Society assists people with hemophilia and related conditions through research, care, advocacy, education, and peer support.

THE NATIONAL HEMOPHILIA FOUNDATION
110 Greene St., Suite 303
New York, NY 10012
(800)424-2634 English, or Spanish at ext. 3054
(212)431-8541

Through its 46 chapters nationwide, the National Hemophilia Foundation offers community and patient services (including camps), public and professional education, hemophilia and AIDS/HIV education and support activities, government relations efforts, and support for research.

Injury

NATIONAL INJURY INFORMATION CLEARINGHOUSE
(301)504-0424

Kidney

NATIONAL KIDNEY AND UROLOGIC DISEASE INFORMATION CLEARING-HOUSE
(301)468-6345

NATIONAL KIDNEY FOUNDATION, INC.
30 East 33rd St.
New York, NY 10016
(800)622-9010
(212)889-2210

More than 20 million Americans have some form of kidney or urologic disease. The National Kidney Foundation works to support prevention, treatment, and cure. It has programs in research, professional education, patient and community services, and organ donation. It has a number of special publications and videos especially targeted toward children who have kidney disease and their parents.

POLYCYSTIC KIDNEY RESEARCH FOUNDATION
922 Walnut St.
Kansas City, MO 64106
(800)PKD-CURE
(816)421-1869

The Polycystic Kidney Research Foundation promotes research to determine the cause, improve clinical treatment, and discover a cure for polycystic kidney disease—the nation's number-one hereditary disease. The Foundation supports research and education for the patients, their families, and communities.

THE KIDNEY FOUNDATION OF CANADA
5160, boul. Decarie, bur. 780
Montreal, Quebec H3X 2H9
Canada
(800)361-7494 (Canada only)
(514)368-4806

The Kidney Foundation of Canada is a national volunteer organization that funds research, provides services for the special needs of individuals living with kidney disease, advocates for access to high-quality health care, and actively promotes awareness and commitment to organ donation.

Lungs

AMERICAN LUNG ASSOCIATION
1740 Broadway
New York, NY 10019
(800)LUNG-USA

The American Lung Association fights lung disease through research, education, community service, and advocacy. Programs of special interest to families whose children have disabilities include "Open Airway," which helps children learn how to manage their asthma, and Asthma Camps which are offered nationally. The toll-free phone number above will automatically put you in touch with your nearest American Lung Association office.

LUNG ASSOCIATION NATIONAL OFFICE
1900 City Park Dr., Suite 508
Gloucester, Ontario K1J 1A3
Canada
(613)747-6776

The Lung Association National Office coordinates the efforts of local and provincial Lung Association offices to help families get the assistance they need to help loved ones who have all kinds of lung disease. Local offices have regionally based activities of interest to children including childhood asthma management programs.

NATIONAL HEART, LUNG, AND BLOOD INSTITUTE
(301)251-1222

Muscular Dystrophy

MUSCULAR DYSTROPHY ASSOCIATION
3300 East Sunrise Dr.
Tucson, AZ 85718
(800)572-1717
(602)529-2000

The Muscular Dystrophy Association is a voluntary health agency—a dedicated partnership between scientists and concerned citizens aimed at conquering 40 neuromuscular diseases that affect more than a million Americans. MDA combats neuromuscular diseases through programs of worldwide research, comprehensive patient and community services (including clinics, equipment purchases, and camps), and far-reaching professional and public health education.

MUSCULAR DYSTROPHY ASSOCIATION OF CANADA
150 Egliniton Ave. E., Suite 400
Toronto, ON M4P 1E8
Canada
(800)567-2873 (Canada only)
(416)488-0030

The Muscular Dystrophy Association of Canada is much like its U.S. counterpart except that it does not offer the clinics. Also see SPINAL MUSCULAR ATROPHY.

Neurologically Disabled

ASSOCIATION FOR THE NEUROLOGICALLY DISABLED OF CANADA
59 Clement Rd.
Etobicoke, ON M9R 1Y5
Canada
(416)244-1992

AND sponsors a home functional rehabilitation service utilizing state-of-the-art techniques to assist families dealing with neurological disabilities (including traumatic brain injury, cerebral palsy, organic brain syndrome, etc.) in obtaining the support and skills necessary to effectively manage their difficulties. A fee is charged for this service and AND is operated privately by Canadian families who work to keep costs to a minimum.

Osteogenesis Imperfecta

OSTEOGENESIS IMPERFECTA FOUNDATION
5005 W. Laurel St., Suite 210
Tampa, FL 33607
(813)282-1161

The Osteogenesis Imperfecta Foundation puts its emphasis on service for families dealing with this condition. It offers publications and videos and has some support groups. In addition, it works to educate the medical community and support medical research.

Ostomy

UNITED OSTOMY ASSOCIATION
36 Executive Park, Suite 120
Irvine, CA 92714
(800)826-0826
(714)660-8624

The United Ostomy Association assists children who have ostomies and their parents with publications and activities through their approximately 400 chapters. Of special interest is their Youth Rally, a three-day event held every year for ostomy patients who are ages 12 through 17.

Paralysis

AMERICAN PARALYSIS ASSOCIATION
500 Morris Ave.
Springfield, NJ 07081
(800)526-3456 24-hour-a-day Hotline (see below)
(800)225-0292
(201)379-2690

Through its Hotline, the Association offers information and referral service for the spinal cord injured, their families, and professionals in the field. It also supports scientific research into ways to cure the disability caused by spinal cord injury as well as sponsoring scientific conferences around the world.

Rare Disorders

NATIONAL ORGANIZATION FOR RARE DISORDERS, INC.
100 Rt. 37
P.O. Box 8923
New Fairfield, CT 06812
(800)999-NORD
(203)746-6518

The National Organization for Rare Disorders, Inc., was created by a group of voluntary agencies, medical researchers, and individuals concerned about Orphan Diseases (affecting fewer than 200,000 people) and Orphan Drugs (medications being developed for these small populations). It supports research, educates the public and medical profession, and acts as a clearinghouse for information about rare disorders as well as network families with similar disorders together for mutual support.

Sickle Cell Disease

SICKLE CELL DISEASE ASSOCIATION OF AMERICA, INC.
3345 Wilshire Blvd., Suite 1106
Los Angeles, CA 90010
(800)421-8453
(213)736-5455

The Sickle Cell Disease Association of America, Inc. works to educate the public and professionals about the problems related to sickle cell conditions which occur in persons of African-American descent. Through its local affiliates in the U.S. and Canada, it offers screening programs to motivate persons of childbearing age to have a sickle cell test and obtain genetic counseling if the test results are positive. Depending on local needs, affiliates may offer other services including referrals and follow-up for medical care and social work services, home nursing care, blood donations, transportation, personal counseling, tutorial programs, career counseling, scholarships, summer camp, and financial aid to meet expenses for medications, food, clothing, or housing.

Spina Bifida

ASSOCIATION FOR SPINA BIFIDA AND HYDROCEPHALUS
42 Park Rd
Peterborough PEI 2UQ
England
Phone: 0733 555988
The Association sends trained field workers to visit families whose children have spina bifida to advise on mobility, continence, and education concerns.

SCOTTISH SPINA BIFIDA ASSOCIATION
190 Queensferry Rd.
Edinburgh EH4 2BW
Scotland
The goal of the Association is to assist children who have spina bifida and their families as well as increase public awareness of the needs of persons who have this diagnosis.

SPINA BIFIDA ASSOCIATION OF AMERICA
4590 MacArthur Blvd. N.W., Suite 250
Washington, D.C. 20007
(800)621-3141
(202)944-3285
Spina bifida is the most frequently occurring, permanently disabling birth defect. Through its approximately 100 local chapters, the Spina Bifida Association of America works to provide information related to spina bifida, including progress in the areas of medicine, education, legislation, and financial support to help fund research into the causes, effects, and treatment of spina bifida. It also encourages the training of professionals involved in treatment.

SPINA BIFIDA ASSOCIATION OF CANADA
#220-389 Donald St.
Winnipeg, Manitoba R3B 2J4
Canada
(800)565-9488 (Canada only)
(204)957-1784

The Spina Bifida Association of Canada's goal is to improve the quality of life of all individuals with spina bifida and/or hydrocephalus and their families through personal support, research, advocacy, and awareness programs.

Spinal Cord Injury

AMERICAN PARALYSIS ASSOCIATION
500 Morris Ave.
Springfield, NJ 07081
(800)225-0292

While the main thrust of the Association is to raise funds for research to cure spinal cord injuries, it also has a special Hotline at (800) 526-3456 where peer counselors who are paralyzed by spinal cord injury (not birth defects) can refer parents to assistance in their area.

NATIONAL SPINAL CORD INJURY ASSOCIATION
600 W. Cummings Park, Suite 2000
Woburn, MA 01801
(800)962-9629
(617)935-2722

The National Spinal Cord Injury Association works to improve standards of care, fund research for cures aimed at minimizing spinal cord damage, and help individuals who have spinal cord injury deal with their new situation and achieve independence. Of special interest is their "In Touch With Kids" support program that provides an opportunity for sharing ideas, feelings, resources, and innovative problem-solving techniques with other families. There is a modest membership fee to join "In Touch With Kids."

Spinal Muscular Atrophy

FAMILIES OF SPINAL MUSCULAR ATROPHY
P.O. Box 1465
Highland Park, IL 60035-7465
(708)432-5551

SMA supports families through information and networking as well as raises funds to promote research into the causes and cure of Spinal Muscular Atrophies. Also see MUSCULAR DYSTROPHY.

Tourette Syndrome

TOURETTE SYNDROME ASSOCIATION, INC.
42-40 Bell Blvd.
Bayside, NY 11361-2874
(718)224-2999

The goals of the Tourette Syndrome Association, Inc., are to educate physicians and the general public about Tourette Syndrome with a view toward promoting more accurate diagnosis and more effective treatment; stimulate and support research to find the cause, a cure, and better means of treatment; be of service to patients and their families; and raise funds to support these goals.

Turner's Syndrome

THE TURNER'S SYNDROME SOCIETY
7777 Keele St., Floor 2
Concord, ON L4K 1Y7
Canada
(800)465-6744 (Canada)
(905)660-7766

The Turner's Syndrome Society of Canada is run by Turner's individuals and their families and supported by professionals. It offers services (including support groups) and disseminates up-to-date medical information to families, physicians, and the general public.

TURNER'S SYNDROME SOCIETY OF THE U.S.
15500 Wayzata Blvd. #768-214
12 Oak Ctr.
Wayzata, MN 55391
(800)365-9944
(612)475-9944

Membership in the Turner's Syndrome Society of the U.S. includes girls and adult women with Turner's Syndrome (which characteristically results in short stature and incomplete sexual maturation without treatment). The Society offers up-to-date information on medical research and treatments, conferences, advocacy, and public relations. On a local level, chapters provide support groups, social activities, and educational forums.

Ventilator- and Technology-Dependent Children

INTERNATIONAL VENTILATOR USERS NETWORK
5100 Oakland Ave., #206
St. Louis, MO 63110
(314)534-0475

The International Ventilator Users Network is a worldwide network of ventilator users and health professionals experienced in and committed to home care and long-term mechanical ventilation. Through its biannual newsletter which is published by the Gazette International Networking Institute (same address), it offers networking as well as information to families on psychosocial adjustments, equipment and techniques, travel, ethical issues, medical topics, and resources.

Werdnig-Hoffmann

See MUSCULAR DYSTROPHY AND SPINAL MUSCULAR ATROPHY.

Computer Bulletin Boards

DISABILITY INFORMATION SERVICES OF CANADA
Ste. 304, 501-18th Ave. S.W.
Calgary, AB T2S 0C7
Canada
(403)244-2836

The Disability Information Services of Canada offers a computer network including TTY & Braille to paid members. The network includes electronic mail capability and computer conferencing.

LINCS (LOCAL INTERAGENCY NETWORK COMMUNICATION)
535 Race St., Suite 140
San Jose, CA 95126
(408)288-5010
(408)294-6933 (Modem line. Use settings: N-8-1: 2400 baud rate)

LINCS is an on-line Bulletin Board System (BBS) which allows computer users to access a network system through the use of a modem and computer to find resources for children with special needs and their families and locate information on parent or professional training. Parents who do not have access to a computer can receive resource information by calling the regular number and asking for LINCS information.

NATIONAL HANDICAPPED SPORTS ELECTRONIC BULLETIN BOARD
451 Hungerford Dr., Suite 100
Rockville, MD 20850
(301)217-0960
(301)217-9836 (Modem line)

The National Handicapped Sports organization offers information, services, and activities for disabled youth and adults. Their 24-hour bulletin board includes an informational library, message capability, up-to-date schedules, chapter lists, membership information, and event registration packets. There is no charge to use the bulletin board (although long-distance toll charges for your phone may apply).

PAPERCHASE
350 Longwood Ave.
Boston, MA 20115
(800)722-2075
(617)278-3900

PAPERCHASE is an on-line information service that helps you search the MEDLINE, Health Planning and Administration (HEALTH), CANCERLIT, and AIDSLINE databases. Only PaperChase lets you search all four data bases at the same time, automatically eliminating duplicates. There is no monthly subscription fee or minimum charge. For a free demonstration disk, call the 800 number. You can access it directly through your modem (call the 800 number for a local access number), or go through CompuServe (GO PCH at the ! prompt and press <Enter>), Westlaw (Type PC at the database prompt and press <Enter>), or Telenet to Paperchase on Internet (at PCH.BIH.HAR-VARD.EDU). PaperChase is a service of Boston's Beth Israel Hospital, a major teaching hospital of the Harvard Medical School.

General Resources

HOLIDAY CARE SERVICE
2 Old Bank Chambers
Station Road
Horley
Surrey RG6 9HW
England
Helpline: 0293 774535 9 A.M.–6 P.M. Mon.–Fri., answerphone out of hours.

The Holiday Care Service is the United Kingdom's central resource for information about holidays for people who have disabilities and others who have special needs.

MOBILITY INFORMATION SERVICE
National Mobility Centre
Unit 2a
Atcham Estate
Shresbury SY4 4UG
England
Phone: 0743 761889

The Mobility Information Service provides driver assessments, adapted vehicles, and information packets for drivers and passengers who have dis-

abilities. The organization is staffed entirely by persons who have disabilities.

NATIONAL INFORMATION CENTER FOR CHILDREN AND YOUTH WITH
DISABILITIES (NICHCY)
P.O. Box 1492
Washington, D.C. 20013-1492
(800)695-0285 (Voice/TT)

NICHCY is an information clearinghouse that provides free information on
disabilities and disability-related issues. It focuses on children and youth
from birth to age 22 and helps them, their parents, and other interested
people with questions about specific disabilities, early intervention, special
education, Individualized Education Programs, and legal issues. NICHCY
also offers referrals to other national organizations and prepared information packets and publications on current issues. Materials are available in
alternative formats and in Spanish.

RADAR (The Royal Association for Disability and Rehabilitation)
12 City Forum
250 City Rd.
London ECIV 8AF
England
Information Line: 071 250 3222

RADAR works to remove the architectural, economic, and attitudinal barriers faced by persons who have disabilities in the areas of mobility, education, social services, housing, and social security.

SHRINERS HOSPITALS FOR CRIPPLED CHILDREN
2900 Rocky Point Dr.
Tampa, FL 33607
(800)237-5055
(800)282-9161 (in Florida)
(800)361-7256 (Canada only)

Children from infancy to their 18th birthday who need treatment for
orthopedic problems, severe burns, or spinal cord injuries can be eligible
for treatment at the 22 Shriners Hospitals in the U.S., Canada, and Mexico if,
in the opinion of the hospital's chief of staff, there is a reasonable possibility
that treatment will benefit the child and if treatment at another facility would
place a financial burden on the patient's family or guardian. You and your
child do not need to know or be related to a Shriner to receive services from
their hospitals.

STOMP (Specialized Training of Military Parents)
12208 Pacific Hwy. S.W.
Tacoma, WA 98499
(206)588-1741 (Voice and TDD)

STOMP, a parent-directed project, exists to empower military parents, individuals with disabilities, and service providers with knowledge, skills, and resources so that they might access services to create a collaborative environment for family and professional partnerships without regard to geographic location. Parents can call STOMP collect from anywhere in the U.S. or overseas for help with their child's educational needs, help with working effectively with military systems like CHAMPUS and the EFMP (Exceptional Family Member Program) for their branch of the service, or for help with other concerns.

TECHNICAL RESOURCE CENTRE
200 1201-5 Street S.W.
Calgary, Alberta T2R 0Y6
Canada
(403)262-9445

The Technical Resource Centre is committed to enhancing the lives of people with physical disabilities by providing information, education, and access to advanced technology through; an assessment and training service, a lending library of devices (including adapted toys and communication aids), a lending library of books and videotapes, and an information service.

Appendix 3

Accessing Government Programs

There are many government programs available to help you with the special needs you face because of your child's disability. Some programs may pay for medical and/or respite care, give referrals to local resources, and even provide funding to help meet certain specific needs. It may take some patience to get through the bureaucracy, so be prepared for that.

Federal Government

Your family may be eligible for a monthly check from the federal government through the Supplemental Security Income (SSI) program. You may have heard of this program assisting retired persons, but it is also available to people (including children) who are blind or have a disability.

SSI benefits are payable to children with disabilities under the age of 18 who have limited income and resources or who come from homes with limited income and resources. The level of payment varies from state to state and can go up every year based on cost-of-living increases.

If your child is under age 18, SSI considers the parents' income and assets when deciding if the child qualifies. You will need to call Social Security at (800) 772–1213 to find out the current levels of income and assets that qualify as well as the amount of the check your child may be eligible to receive.

While your local Social Security office decides if your child's income and assets are within the SSI limits, all documents and evidence pertaining to the disability are sent to a state office, usually called the Disability Determination Service (DDS). There, a team comprised of a disability evaluation specialist and a doctor reviews your child's case to decide if he or she meets the SSI definition of disability.

If the existing records are not thorough enough for the DDS team to make a decision, you may be asked to take your child to a special examination that Social Security will pay for.

The law states that a child will be considered disabled if he or she is not working and has an impairment that is as severe as one that would disable an adult. This means the condition must limit the child's ability to function like other children of the same age so much that the impairment is comparable to one that would make an adult disabled.

If your child has a diagnosis, that diagnosis will be checked against a specific listing of impairments that is contained in Social Security's regulations. If your child does not have a firm diagnosis or the diagnosis does not appear on the listing, the symptoms, signs, and/or laboratory findings of the condition are compared to listed conditions to see if they are the same as, or equal to, the conditions listed. If the disability cannot be established using the "listing" criteria, then the disability evaluation team will assess the child's ability to function in everyday life. Children are considered disabled for SSI purposes if their impairment substantially reduces their ability to do the things and behave in the ways that children of a similar age normally do.

The disability-evaluation process normally takes several months. However, you can get funding more quickly if your child's condition is so severe that he or she is presumed to be disabled. In that case, SSI benefits are paid for up to six months while the evaluation process takes place (if your family meets the financial qualifications for SSI). If you receive these special payments and SSI later determines that your child's disability is not severe enough to qualify for the program, you will not have to repay the money.

The conditions that automatically qualify your child for SSI payments (again, if you meet the financial tests) include:

AIDS	Blindness
Deafness*	Cerebral Palsy*
Down Syndrome	Muscular Dystrophy*
Diabetes (with amputation of one foot)	
Amputation of two limbs	
Amputation of leg at the hip	
Significant mental deficiency	

Remember, when your child turns 18, SSI no longer considers the parents' income and assets to determine whether your child can qualify for SSI. If your child continues to live with you and does not pay for food or shelter after her 18th birthday, she may still qualify, but get a lower payment rate.

*In some cases.

The reason to remember this is that you may find it very helpful for your child to have this income if he or she plans to go to college or get other post-high-school training, although the money is not in any way tied to continuing education.

Government Contacts, by State

The toll-free telephone numbers listed here can put you in touch with referrals to appropriate medical specialists, available resources, and programs and other services in the United States. They can be helpful if you are just starting or if you are further along and just want to check for possible resources you might not be aware of. Some states offer additional specialized 800 numbers that are also included.

In addition, consider calling the National Information Clearinghouse for Infants with Disabilities and Life-Threatening Conditions for further referrals or if your state is not listed below. They can be reached at (800) 922-9234, ext. 201.

State	Information & Referral Number
• Arkansas	(800) 482-5850
• Colorado	(800) 688-7777 Baby Care (800) 255-3477 Disability Referral Services
• Connecticut	(800) 286-2229
• Delaware	(800) 464-4357 United Way of Delaware
• Florida	(800) 825-5736
• Georgia	(800) 822-2539
• Hawaii	(800) 235-5477 Zero to Three
• Idaho	(800) 926-2588 Careline
• Illinois	(800) 322-3722
• Indiana	(800) 433-0746
• Iowa	(800) 779-2001
• Kansas	(800) 332-6262 Make a Difference Line
• Kentucky	(800) 232-1160
• Louisiana	(800) 922-3425 Disabilities Information Access Line
• Maine	(800) 698-3624
• Maryland	(800) 456-8900

- Massachusetts (800) 882-1435
  (800) 462-5015
- Michigan (800) 359-3722
  (800) 788-7889 TDD
- Minnesota (800) 728-5420
- Mississippi (800) 844-0898
- Missouri (800) 878-6246
- Montana (800) 762-9891
- Nebraska (800) 358-8802
- Nevada (800) 992-0900, ext. 4885
- New Hampshire (800) 852-3345, ext. 4488
- New Jersey
- New Mexico (800) 552-8195 Developmental Disabilities
  Planning Council
- New York (800) 522-5006 Growing Up Healthy Hotline
- North Carolina (800) TLC-0042
- North Dakota (800) 472-2436
- Oklahoma (800) 522-0323
- Oregon (800) 452-3563
- Pennsylvania (800) 852-4453
- Rhode Island (800) 346-1004 Family Health Information Line
- South Carolina (800) 868-0404 Careline
- South Dakota (800) 658-3080
- Tennessee (800) 428-2229
  (800) 852-7517 Early Intervention System
- Texas (800) 252-8823
- Utah (800) 826-9662
- Vermont (800) 660-4427
- Virginia (800) 523-4019
- Washington (800) 841-1410
- West Virginia (800) 642-8522
- Wisconsin (800) 441-4576
- Wyoming (800) 842-8333

For Families in the United Kingdom

If you live in the United Kingdom, you should contact the Benefits Agency to find out about any Social Security benefits your family may be eligible for. You can call the DSS Disability Benefits line at 0800 882200 between 8 A.M. and 6:30 P.M. Monday through Friday and from 9 A.M. to 1 P.M. on Saturday. You can also contact the Forms Completion Service for assistance in completing your form at 0800 441144. Families who prefer to call in the Welsh language should call 0800 289011 and families in Northern Ireland should call 0800 616757.

Index

228